Hills of Home

Hills of Home
The Rural Ozarks of Arkansas

Photographs: Roger Minick

Writings: Bob Minick

Drawings & Etchings: Leonard Sussman

Scrimshaw Press
1975

Special thanks to
The John Simon Guggenheim Memorial Foundation
for the Fellowship to complete this photography

LIBRARY OF CONGRESS CATALOGING IN PUBLICATION DATA

Minick, Roger.
  Hills of Home.

  1. Ozark Mountain region—Description and travel—Views.
2. Ozark Mountain region—Social life and customs—Pictorial
works. 3. Ozark Mountain region—Fiction. I. Minick, Bob,
1925-   II. Sussman, Leonard, 1947-   III. Title.
F417.09M56   976.7′1′00222   75-14226
ISBN 0-912020-48-2

The Scrimshaw Press
149 Ninth Street
San Francisco, CA 94103

A Word Before

WHEN HE WAS twelve years old, Roger Minick's family picked up and left a comfortable home in the Arkansas Ozarks and moved to southern California. Coming from a town of some three hundred people, the Minicks made the adjustments for a new life in the sprawl and confusion of a section of Los Angeles. The Ozarks lay behind them and it was not until a few years ago, when he began a photographic project on the Sacramento River delta region near San Francisco, that Roger's faint memories of the hills and small towns of Arkansas began to be recovered. The delta photographs emerged as a book and the next step was virtually predestined—to return to the Ozarks for the photographs you will see in *Hills of Home*.

Every artist is, of course, selective. Roger has chosen to photograph that which is special in a special place—a rural place, in many ways unique, that is steadily giving way to the standardization that is concomitant with modern living. These photographs may deal with one relatively unknown pocket of civilization, but they can be seen as representative of a rural experience in America as a whole. There are many places one can travel in this country and see something of the Ozarks, *some* sign of the essence of small-farm living. In northwest Arkansas, as elsewhere, though much is being lost to urban pressures, five minutes from any hamburger stand one finds *country* and twenty more minutes from there often comes remote country, where a woman may still cook over a wood-burning stove and a man may still plow with a team of mules. It is this more remote,

archetypal, land and life that has, in this particular project, taken hold of Roger's imagination.

Bob Minick, Roger's father, is a native Ozarker and a natural storyteller. For *Hills of Home* he has often drawn upon his own experiences and those from the history of his own family, Ozarkers for three generations back. "Ozark Bride," for instance, is a composite of recollections heard from Bob's own mother, and "Sister Cora" happened just the way it is told. For many of the tales in the book, family experiences have been combined with stories collected throughout the Ozarks and then interwoven with ideas of Bob's own creation.

Leonard Sussman has created his drawings and etchings from the Minick stories and photographs. His primitive and whimsical style has seemed to be compatible with the spirit of Bob's stories and has well served to bind together photographs and text into a whole.

There are two families that continue to appear throughout the body of photographs and each has personal meaning for Roger and me. Roger came to know Agnes and Harrison Pierce during his initial photographic trips to the Ozarks, several years before he and I met. By the time I made my first trip to Arkansas, I knew the Pierce faces and lives so well through Roger's work that I felt *I* was returning home when Mrs. Pierce greeted us at her gate that spring day in 1972.

Mr. Pierce had died the previous January but we detected few changes in the Pierce place when we came calling. They had lived there, after all, some fifty years and it shouldn't have come as a surprise that Mrs. Pierce would continue to live on the farm in the same manner she always had.

Mrs. Pierce is a stout, pleasantly feisty woman in her seventies who handles a pitchfork or an embroidery needle with equal assurance. She says what she thinks and speaks with a tone of authority. When I asked her once whether she was ever afraid to live alone out in the country, she replied only, "No, I have a gun." (And the city visitor was reminded that, indeed, what is to be feared when in the course of a day the only passers-by are the rural mail carrier and the school bus?)

The Pierce home is much like others in the Ozarks—square and wooden with two front doors and a front porch with a pair of ladderback chairs where a person can sit and talk, read the local news, or simply look out across the trees and witness the cycles of the seasons. Inside the house, the floors are covered with floral-patterned linoleum and a bed is found in what might be called the living room. Depending on the season, the heat-stove sits in the living room with chairs gathered about or is stored on the front porch when summer nears. The kitchen table is usually decked out with leftovers from the previous meal, protected under a clean, white tea towel.

Friends will drive Mrs. Pierce into town for supplies and a few groceries and her children help her with the heavy farm work, but otherwise Mrs. Pierce is fairly self-reliant, toting hay-bales, clearing brush, tending the garden each summer. She once proudly told Roger that she had in the cellar enough home-canned goods to take care of Harrison's and her needs for five years.

Over the years Roger gave the Pierces a number of photographs he had made of them and Mrs. Pierce often brings them out to show her guests. Harrison was most pleased with the one showing him watering his prized mules, Jude and John. Though the mules had to be sold when Harrison died, the photograph remains, framed and hanging in the Pierce living room.

In many ways the Pierces lived like the original settlers in the Ozarks—the white settlers who came in to this virgin country and homesteaded after the Louisiana Purchase. Many of them came from the southern Appalachians—rather as "A. Man" and Sarah did—and found the hills of the Ozarks a comfortable reminder of the hills back home. This is a rugged landscape; the Ozarks remained isolated well into the twentieth century and today can claim a number of old-timers who still practice the ways of the past.

What is uncommon today is to find *young* families that practice a traditional and lightly-mechanized farm life. It was Roger's and my good fortune to meet such a family while we were living for a year in the Ozarks.

Eliza and Ed Stilley carry on a tradition which has been passed down to them through generations, a preoccupation with life's necessities and God's preachings and lessons. It is, to an outsider, a demanding life. No one in the Stilley house is ever without work; Eliza and Ed put in a twelve- to sixteen-hour day and the children join in the round of chores as soon as they arrive home from school. Though the family has a truck and car and electricity in the house, they live without indoor plumbing or a telephone or television or other so-called necessities. Eliza cooks on a wood-burning stove, churns her own butter, and she or some other family member has to carry in from the spring all the water used in preparing and cleaning up after a meal and for bathing. Though Ed will occasionally borrow a neighbor's tractor, he performs the bulk of his farm work with horse-drawn equipment (he jokes that his furrows are so crooked that they'd break a snake's back).

Like any farmer, Ed is a walking compendium of home remedies and useful innovations. To keep the cows from kicking over the milk bucket, he ties their tails to a low rafter while he milks. To keep ruts from being cut into their steep road whenever it rains, he sets logs across the road at an angle to divert the water off to one side. He adds salt to the dairy feed for higher milk production, says that blackberry tea cures dysentery and that goldenseal is good for eye disorders.

Ed comes from a long line of hearty people; his grandmother was a farmer and could cut railroad ties with a broadaxe "faster than most men." Although he refers to himself as a mere splinter of a man, he cleared much of their eighty acres with only an axe and a half-crosscut. He admits that he pushes too hard but knows, until the children are older, there is no slowing down.

A few times in recent years Ed has suffered what he guesses is a heart attack. Wherever he was when the attack came, in the cow shed or in the cornfield, Ed simply stopped what he was doing, lay down, prayed, and waited for it to pass.

As for Eliza, perhaps her most prominent characteristic is her candor. From the moment we met, she treated me as the closest of friends, expressing her personal concerns, her concerns for Ed's health and for the family during the times that make money scarce. Eliza is a determined worker; in the summertime she will stand over the hot stove and put up, on the average, forty quarts of green beans, forty quarts of tomatoes and countless jars of other vegetables, jams, fruits and meats—enough to cover many of the family's needs until springtime.

The Stilleys attend church three times a week, Wednesday night and twice on Sunday. Though the trip to church is a long one, the family must return home between the two Sunday services to tend to farm chores. To pass time on these trips, the family sings hymns or has Bible quizzes. Ed, who used to be a preacher, will begin by reciting a passage from Scripture and the children will try to complete it or the children will quiz Ed by choosing lines from the Bible and making him guess where they came from. Eliza says that Ed often guesses the correct book and chapter and occasionally even the correct verse.

The Stilleys normally purchase only four staples at the market: salt, sugar, baking soda and flour. Everything else they have raised themselves except what they can bring in from fishing or hunting squirrels and 'coons on and around the farm. Food is usually plentiful but cash can be scarce, and so twice a week, in the late summer, they drive in to town to peddle vegetables house to house. In the winter they manage by selling milk, eggs, firewood and the rabbits they have raised.

The sort of life the Stilleys lead is, of course, vulnerable to everyday setbacks and disappointments—a fresh batch of milk is bitter, a much-needed calf dies, the cost of feed grain goes up again, a child is bitten by a snake. In the past, it seemed that Ed and Eliza had been spared major catastrophes, but at the end of our year in Arkansas, the Stilleys were told by the dairy company that had been purchasing their milk that their contract would be cancelled unless the Stilleys installed a refrigeration unit and made other improvements in their milk shed, improvements which the Stilleys could not afford. Milk was the family's primary source of income; had they been a larger producer the company would have helped pay for the improvements. Roger and I left Arkansas before this matter was settled, but in correspondence with the family we have learned that they have indeed lost their milk business and Ed has begun working part-time at a saw mill.

There are certain qualities about the Stilley children (and their parents) which I am tempted to link with the kind of life they lead. Besides having lively and inquiring minds, the Stilley children are tremendously observant; anything new or unusual attracts and maintains their interest. One very hot day we were all up in the garden. While Roger was photographing Ed plowing, he found himself running out of film and asked Janie, age six, if she'd mind bringing him another roll from his case in the barn. Minutes later she was running back toward us with her hands held in front of her and tightly cupping the roll of film. We were puzzled by her intent manner until she said she was protecting the film from the sun; we realized she must have remembered some passing comment of Roger's from long before that film is light- and heat-sensitive. Janie was, as were all the children, fascinated with Roger's camera equipment, always insisting to know how it all worked. When I once asked Janie if she remembered everything she was told, she answered, very simply, "Yes, except what I don't understand in the first place." And that was that.

It is difficult to imagine how the Stilley children will feel about the farm when they are grown. Eliza told me with a smile that Nathan, her youngest son, says that he prefers school in the large nearby town to being at home because, he grumbles, when he's at home he has to work. On the other hand, Martha, the oldest daughter, once said to me she would simply *have* to marry a farmer because she couldn't *stand* to live without chickens and rabbits around. Whatever path the Stilley children choose when they are adults, there will likely be difficult choices to make. I can only wish them well and hope that they remain, in some way, close to their hills of home.

JOYCE MINICK

Dedicated to the Stilleys: Ed, Eliza,
Martha, Steven, Oscar, Nathan and Janie

20

21

24

34

36

Sister Cora

I REMEMBERED SISTER CORA from my childhood. I remembered her daughter, too. It was their hair that caused me to remember them. The picture I had of them in my memory was exactly like the photograph I found of them among my mother's old portraits. They were together, mother and daughter, the mother standing, the daughter seated. The mother was gently brushing the daughter's beautiful auburn hair. Her hair was a cloud of glory that spilled out on the floor to intertwine perfectly with that of her mother's. Surely these were daughters of Absalom with hair longer than their bodies and of such mystical beauty as to remain alive in one's mind for a lifetime.

I tried to recall something else about them other than their hair, but it was of no use. When I thought of them, I thought of their hair—long and wavy, vital and beautiful—identical hair. I knew that our seeing them, when I was a child, had something to do with going to church, but I did not remember seeing Sister Cora and her daughter at church. I remembered them only before church, during revivals or camp meetings, when they would brush and comb their hair in preparation for going into the presence of God to worship. Sister Cora's hair was her glory. She wore her hair for the glory of her God. It was doubtful to me if any priest, rabbi, or holy man or woman in all of the history of mankind ever practiced a more painstaking and meaningful ritual in preparation for worship than did Sister Cora when she balled up her hair for the meetings.

Since I remembered Sister Cora as somewhat older than my mother, I was surprised that day when my mother told us Sister Cora was still alive and living by herself on their old home place. The very next morning Roger and I were on our way to see Sister Cora.

I couldn't recall ever having been to Sister Cora's home. But, except for its state of general disrepair, it was very much as I remembered so many of the old home places of my childhood in the Ozarks. There was the bungalow with a full porch across the front. A porch swing, two leather-bottomed rocking chairs, a sagging gate held shut with a ball and chain of Civil War vintage, remnants of some child's rope swing dangling from a gnarled oak, firewood piled along the fence, chickens scratching among chips and hollyhocks—these scenes, like pages from an old and familiar book, swept across my vision as we approached the old place.

An old dog came out to meet us, barking viciously at one end while wagging a friendly tail at the other. There was an old oaken bucket gone to staves hanging at the well. Long before the first electric pump had been put in, that oaken bucket had been replaced by a series of lighter galvanized ones. These were gone now, as were the first two pumps, rusting away in a pile of junk just outside the fence. But the old oaken bucket remained. It seemed to be waiting for something, possibly for an era to end, for history to repeat itself. "Heaven and earth shall pass away . . ." but old oaken buckets, gourd dippers, rock cellars and well houses and smokehouses live on . . .

Old smokehouses. . . . This one had been built in two stages. The lower story was built of hewn logs weatherproofed with red clay dirt. Even the scarred roots of the great white oak had not been able to destroy this structure though it had been lifted several inches at one corner. The upper story looked as if it had been built before steel nails and was a mere skeleton of its former self. All that remained were bits of the roof here and there held up by some of the heavier structural framing. Hanging from these exposed rafters were old bits of rusty baling wire and binder twine from which had hung, in bygone years, choice hams, shoulders, sowbelly, and assortments of possum hides, skunk hides, coon hides, and clusters of onions and red peppers.

Little children must have once played "house" or "church" here and been forever infused with the pungent smell of cured ham, salt pork, burning hickory, skunk grease and animal hides. Possibly one of those children had been me. I couldn't be sure. As a child I may have swung high in that swing there in that old oak or climbed up among the lightning-scarred branches of the giant tree. One or more of my toenails might have been lost to the exposed roots. I had probably laughed and cried right here at this spot when I was too young to remember. It just plain seemed to me that I had.

When Sister Cora came out on the porch to see what the dog was barking about, we introduced ourselves. Yes, she remembered me. Yes, she seemed glad to see us and asked us to set a spell.

I told Sister Cora why we had come: that I wanted to see her hair again and that my son, Roger, was a photographer, and wanted to take pictures of her—with her hair down, if possible. She seemed a bit suspicious.

I tried to convey to her the beautiful memories I had carried of her all my life. She seemed pleased, not in a vain sense,

but humbly pleased, as one who is glad that others have appreciated a woman's God-given glory.

Her hair was balled back so I couldn't tell if it was still so long that it brushed on the floor when she walked. Yes, she said, her hair was as long as ever. It still reached the floor standing up. "No, there ain't many women could say that their hair had never been sheared nor shorn." Even her daughter couldn't say that anymore, she told us. "Been too much trouble," she said, "but it ain't never too much trouble to live by the Bible, and the Bible says that a woman's hair is her glory and that even nature itself teaches that a woman ought to have long hair. You still believe the word of God don't you, Bobby?" No one had called me Bobby for a long while. I tried to change the subject, but failed.

"I believe in living by the Bible. It is the only book we need. You search this house over and over and the Bible is the only book you will find here," she continued. "You was called to preach, warn't you? Are you preaching now?"

"No, I'm a schoolteacher," I answered.

"You can't get away from the calling of God. His callings are without repentance. The Bible is plain on that, you know. Now you was saying you wanted to take my picture. What did you want a picture of me for? So you could take it out to California so them people could laugh at this crazy old woman?"

Roger tried to assure her that this was not the intent. He told her that she was a beautiful and rare person and it was for this reason that he wanted her picture.

"I might of been all right once, but that was before I got so old and lost my eye."

I had noticed that she had often put her hand over her eye and turned her face to one side. "You're about the same age as my mother aren't you?" I asked.

"Oh no, I'm six years older than Nora. I'll be ninety next year, if the Lord tarries."

"That is remarkable," was all I could say.

"But I don't know why the Lord let me lose my eye. I just don't understand it."

"Things just happen," I said, "I'm sure that it's nothing you've done. . . ."

"I've searched my life and I just can't think what it is I've done that would have caused this to happen."

"What happened?" Roger asked. Sister Cora obviously wanted to talk about it.

"Well, I got this cow I was keeping here for milk and she kept getting out of the pasture. So I decided that I would try to fix the fence. When I got back from mending the fence I had a lot of wire left over. So I picked up this old nail. It was one of them old square iron nails like we used to use, sort of like a spike. I was gonna hammer it into that old log barn to hang my wire on. Well, I held the nail up with one hand and went to hit it with the other. I had this ball-peen hammer and I must of hit with the wrong end or hit at a slant or something, for when I hit it that spike flew right out of my hand and knocked my eye right out."

"Knocked it out?" Roger exclaimed.

"Yes, it was hanging, and I carried it across to the field over there to where my daughter lives."

"You walked all the way over there carrying your eye?" Roger couldn't believe this and neither could I.

"Oh yes, but it is only about half a mile."

"What did you do then?" Roger inquired.

"They made me go to a doctor. I didn't want to. If I'd gone to the doctor before I lost my eye, I'd of thought that was it."

"What do you mean?" Roger asked.

"I'd of thought that that was what I was being punished for. I never took any medicine or rubbed anything on—I still ain't. God is my healer. He's took care of me. Doctor couldn't do anything nohow. Said my eye was too damaged. 'Course it was. I knew that already. The Lord had taken it. 'The Lord giveth and the Lord taketh away. Blessed be the name of the Lord.' But I can't figure out what I done that the Lord took my eye. Before, I could always figure it out what it was that I was doing wrong."

"You had something like this happen before?" Roger asked.

"It was about forty years ago when I had appendicitis. I was dying, they said. They all wanted me to get a doctor. I told the Lord I'd die first. And I told the Lord that if He wanted to take me away from my husband and the children, just to go right ahead and do it, but if He didn't want to and would show me what it was that I was doing wrong, I would stop doing it no matter what it was. And He showed me what it was. I liked to read novels. I was always reading them novels. The Lord just showed me all them novels that I had been reading. Just brought them up before me one at a time: *A Girl of the Limberlost*, *The Winning of Barbara Worth*, *Shepherd of the Hills*, *When a Man's a Man*, *The Trail of the Lonesome Pine*, *The Little Shepherd of Kingdom Come*, *Riders of the Purple Sage* ... all them books just came up before my eyes like a picture. So I knowed that the Lord wanted me to give up reading them books. That was what I liked to do mostly—just read them stories. So I promised the Lord that if He would let me live and take care of my family that I would give up them stories. And He healed me! I ain't read anything 'cepting the Bible for nigh on forty years...."

Roger busied himself taking pictures of Sister Cora. It was plain that she was enjoying it, but she continued to express misgivings occasionally....

"You ain't gonna take these out to California so people can laugh, are you? I hear tell that they made a picture show poking fun at how we live here in these hills. 'Course I ain't never seen no picture show. Been a Christian since I was old enough."

Roger had her posing, standing in the weeds down near the henhouse, her hair falling down about her to the ground. The old dog waited anxiously nearby, apparently disturbed by the strange goings-on. Some bronco-looking horses came up from a pasture behind the henhouse and tried to nuzzle Sister Cora over the gate. A hen cackled, announcing the arrival of a new egg, and a banty came clucking through the weeds with her brood of awkward half-breed chicks. Next to the chopping block, among the hollyhocks, several Plymouth Rock hens cleaned their feathers in the dust of the old chipyard. A Rhode Island Red rooster flew atop a nearby post and crowed his approval of the happy state of the world. Somewhere out of sight a cowbell tinkled, and closer by one could hear the steady cadence of a sow grunting as she gave down her milk and nursed her pigs.

She belongs here, I thought, here with her dog, her hens, rocking chair, hollyhocks, rain barrels, quilting frames and old brindle cow. Who in the world, I wondered, would poke fun at a ninety-year-old woman with all of that?

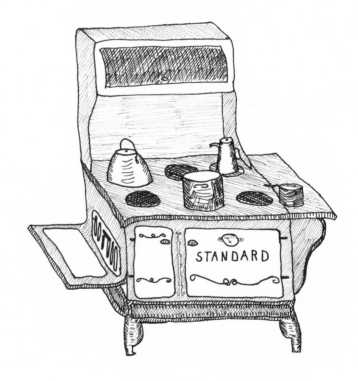

Ozark Bride
(As told by the bride 70 years later)

THE FIRST TIME I remember seeing George was when his dad, Tuck, brought all seven of them boys to town to buy winter clothes. They was a big family, seven boys and seven girls. They was hanging all over that team and wagon. I remember seeing George, so pitiful-like, among all them others, standing there on the tongue of the wagon between the horses. Seemed more bashful and shy than them others. I remember the others teasing him and calling him "Poker," 'cause he stood and sat so straight, you know. So I felt sorry for him. 'Course George never did like for me to tell that. He never did like to be called Poker either. 'Course folks was always doing it just 'cause George didn't want them to. People was always teasing him. I think when he got older he enjoyed all that attention though.

Well anyway they came to town and Tuck lined all them boys up on a bench out in front of the General Mercantile Store on the porch and the storekeeper brought out a big pile of number-eight shoes. Shoes didn't come in boxes then like they do today. Tuck bought sixteen of them shoes. Them shoes wasn't paired then like shoes is now. They wasn't no right shoe or no left shoe. Every shoe was cut the same.

It was late fall and already getting cold so Tuck had them boys to all put them shoes on. That was some sight, all them setting there in shoes just alike, their toes all slanting out catawhampas-like. There was Mary, their old-maid aunt, setting there bossing them and they was looking like a bunch of scared chickens on a roost. I never did like that Mary—from the first time I laid eyes on her I could tell what she was like.

The next time I saw George was at this gathering at a schoolhouse. We was playing Snaps. 'Course you don't know what Snaps is. Well it is sort of like playing Drop the Handkerchief. Well, I guess I done it 'cause I felt sorry for him. George got all embarrassed and stood so straight that he almost fell over backward.

The first time George walked me home he didn't really ask me. He just sort of sidled up to me and started walking along. It was about two miles to my house and we'd no more than got started than a rabbit jumped out in front of us. George said, "Do you like rabbit?" I said I did. We walked on for another thirty minutes or so and nothing else was said until just before we got home George said, "And the gravy is sure good too, ain't it?" That was all he said the whole walk.

First time he ate Sunday dinner with us we had breaded tomatoes—lots of people didn't eat tomatoes in them days. When we passed them to George he asked what they was and we told him and he says he don't know if he likes them or not but all the time he is dipping them out on his plate till he had 'bout half of them. Papa says, "Well, George, why don't you just take a little of them till you see if you like them?"

One time he was eating with us and he had his plate all loaded down with stuff—he always took a way more than he ought to. This time he had a big pickle on his plate and he tried to cut it with the side of his fork (he never used a knife) and the pickle slipped out from under his fork and knocked all that food off his plate across our white tablecloth. George was wearing a white shirt and it was the first white shirt he ever wore. Well he was so nervous by this time that he looked down in his lap and saw the edge of that white tablecloth and thought it was his shirttail so he tucked it in his pants and when he got up from the table he drug half the table right off on the floor.

In time George got up some confidence in himself and one night him and some other boys rode up and down the road in front of our place shooting their guns off. Papa saw George in town after that and told him he'd best stop disturbing the peace or he was gonna get throwed in jail and George got sassy with Papa and said, "They got to catch me first." "Oh, they'll catch you soon enough," Papa said. So after that for a while Dad wouldn't let George come to the house. But George kept trying to come over, acting meek as a kitten. That one shooting spree was about the total of George's sowing wild oats.

Courting was different then than it is nowadays. There was always old folks around. Papa would always follow along behind when a boy was walking me home from church or something. He'd always make me keep the door opened when a boy came to see me. We had something called a love seat that we used to set on and Papa would make me keep that placed where he could see it from where he sat in the other room. Sometimes I would move it before a boy came over but Papa would always come in and move it back to where he could see us. 'Course none of this kept George away. He always said I got a hold of him and just hung on.

When George asked me to marry him he went "tee-hee." He was just that green. We wasn't nothing but children. I don't know why we got married so young. I guess there wasn't nothing else to do. George forgot how old he was. I think he was ashamed of how young he was. I wore a blue dress and Papa cried.

Then we lived for about a week or so with Tuck. That week with George's dad and his sister Mary almost drove me crazy. They gave us the worst bed in the house. This was Mary's doings. The bed fell in in the middle of the first night and Mary accused George of jumping up and down on it. 'Course that embarrassed George more than anything.

I remember that first night before we went to bed I knelt down beside the bed and George wanted to know what I was doing and I told him I was praying. He wanted to know what I was doing that for and I told him I thought I was gonna need all the help I could get.

George and Mary was always fighting. Mary ran the house with a iron hand. She gave us linsey-wool quilts to sleep next to and I couldn't stand them. I was used to sleeping on sheets. But George couldn't sleep on sheets. It is a wonder that we ever made it together.

The first thing Tuck said to me when George brought me home was, "Do you know how to do anything?" Then pretty soon he brings me some of George's old britches for me to mend and I was so nervous that I forgot to tie a knot in the thread and when I pulled the thread it came right out through the cloth, and Tuck said, "Just as I thought, you don't know how to do anything!" Then he grabbed them up and took them to Mary to do. They was always telling me to do something, wouldn't wait to see if I was gonna do it, and then when I did something they would do it over again. I'd make coffee and they would throw it out and make it over. Mary told me to make some pies and then she stood right over me to see that I done it the way she wanted me to, trying to make me feel like I couldn't do anything. They was fruit pies and when I started to put sugar in the fillings Mary said no, I couldn't do that, you was supposed to put sugar only in the crust. Well, I said I wouldn't make it any other way and walked out. Mary's pies was always terrible and I felt sorry for George having to grow up eating them kind of pies. George always liked my pies.

Mary wouldn't let me make George's lunch when George went out to work in the fields. "While he's still in this house I'll do it," Mary said. But George wouldn't eat it and Mary would get real mad when George brought it back. Once they got in a fight over it at the supper table and Mary got mad and throwed a fork at George. It missed him and stuck in a door. Mary said a bad word and Tuck said, "If you say that again I'll knock your block off."

Finally I couldn't stand it no more so I told George I want to leave but Tuck wants us to stay but only because he wants George to help out in the fields and me help out in the house. Tuck always had to have all the help in the world. He couldn't do nothing by himself. When he went to the field he'd take all seven of them boys with him. When they was gathering corn, instead of doing it by the row like anyone else, Tuck would take all seven of them boys around in one wagon and go to the top side of the field and come around the side of the hill in a circle gathering the corn. Well I couldn't stand it no more and I told George I would go back home if he didn't take me somewhere else to live. 'Course I couldn't of done that for Papa would of said, "You made your bed now lay in it."

Tuck said that since we was gonna leave he would take us to Berryville and buy us some things we was gonna need to set up housekeeping. I was all excited about getting some stuff of my own. It took us most all day to get to Berryville and all the way we noticed flags being flown. When we got there everything was closed. It was some kind of a holiday. So we had to go back another day. We finally got there and I started going around picking out the things I thought I needed. But everytime I'd pick out something Tuck would say, "No, you don't need that, we got a extra bedstead you can have. No, you don't need to buy that, we got a extra stove you can have. No, we got a extra dresser at home for you. No, we got a extra kettle."

Pretty soon Tuck goes off and leaves me with one of his granddaughters and says, "Now you all look some more and make up your minds what you want. Then you come on over to the grocery store and I'll buy your lunches." 'Course George is off to himself 'cause he can't stand what's been happening. We look some more and then go over to the grocery store for our lunches. By now we have got all giggly from the way Tuck is acting. We find Tuck in the back of the store setting on a nail keg sort of hiding behind some sacks of beans. He has got him a box of sodacrackers and is dipping them down in the brown sugar barrel and a-eating them. When he offers them to us we are laughing so hard we blow the sugar off in his face.

After all that going to town to buy an outfit for setting up housekeeping we go back home with only one bucket, one washboard, and one skillet. By the time we get home I'm so upset I'm just bawling. Mary comes out and looks it over and says that we spent too much.

As we're getting ready to leave, Sarah, George's mother, tells Mary to go get us some quilts. But Mary says she ain't gonna get none 'cause George was always scaring her, or pushing her, or teasing her, and causing her to stick her finger with the needle when she was quilting. But Sarah insists, so Mary goes upstairs and comes back with the oldest, raggediest quilt she can find. Sarah gets mad—it was the only time I ever saw her get mad—and she makes Mary go up and get us some better quilts. As she goes to get them she says, "I don't know why George married her. She's so young and she don't know how to do anything." She was always saying that and Tuck said it all the time too.

Mary insists on going with us when we leave. She wants to take us by a farm sale. So we start over to this sale with the buggy loaded down with some of the awfulest hand-me-downs you ever saw. They was awful! All the way in the buggy George and Mary kept quarreling about the stuff we was taking. The way we had to go was along this high bluff. At the highest point Mary grabbed the reins away from George and pulled the horse toward the bluff as hard as she could. George said, "What on earth are you trying to do?" Mary said, "I'm trying to kill Nora!" I thought George was gonna throw Mary off that bluff.

When we got to the sale Mary introduces me to some of the people she knows and says, "This is Nora, she's married to George, she don't know why she married him but she has. They're gonna go live by themselves like grown-ups." I felt about so high. We bought some dishes at the sale and then we went on to this place where we was gonna live. Mary stayed at the sale.

Now that's the way it was when I got married. We didn't have no honeymoon and things like that like they have nowadays. But we made out about as good as most, anyhow.

In the Beginning A Man...

THAT SUMMER WHEN A. Man came up into the highlands of Kentucky and out along the bank of Wide Creek and began to fell twelve-inch oak trees—hewing, notching and hoisting them up, forming the four walls of a sizable cabin—the folks believed that A. Man was doing what comes naturally to any young man.

It had been a bright day for the community of Wide Creek when A. Man first arrived. Of course, no one remembered anything about the young blond giant that day, what with Old Hickory and his band of cutthroats wiping dirty boots on everything in sight. But when Andrew Jackson roared out of town two days later, promising the good people that, once he had become President, he'd "drive the Indians to hell and back," A. Man stayed behind.

A strong, big fellow with a rusty beard and long blond hair, and bright blue eyes which seemed to mirror the waters of the seven seas, A. Man walked like a sailor. Possibly he was a Viking, or maybe a former convict or pirate. He seemed to have no lack of gold as he stocked up on supplies at Bufford Hayes's store.

Log-by-log the house grew, neatly built, corners notched this way and that, old men admitting that they could not have done better. It was a substantial house, this cabin, large enough to house a woman and children. The girls from Wide Creek continued to announce regularly that they would not have anything to do with the man—never—even if he were the last man on earth. But they changed their place for doing laundry to a rock closer to the cabin site and stole anxious glances at A. Man, who, they said, made them feel funny. And at night not a few mountain maidens privately jigged some fancy steps as A. Man's music drifted up through the trees. But young girls had to be careful about such things, for a great Methodist revival had swept the upper Ohio River valley highlands, and dancing, except at the meetings, had become one of the seven deadly sins. A. Man seemed to be oblivious to all this and set about cutting windows and doors into his cabin, fitting rafters, splitting lathing and shingles from the virgin timber and playing his fiddle.

There came a day in late winter when the cabin was all neatly fitted together, complete with hewn log floors, windows (ordered through Bufford Hayes) installed, rough doors made from the best oak and fixed with iron hinges and wooden latches and leather straps hanging outside. It was time to roof the house—to finish it off—a job well done. But on that day the strange man did the strangest of things: very carefully he began to tear the house down. Girls peeking through the blossoming dogwood bushes saw this unusual

53

happening and rushed back to the store at Wide Creek and duly reported the event.

"A. Man is tearing down his house," they said, afraid of what that might mean, for it was a fearful thing to see a man tear down a house that he has worked so hard to build. "Maybe he has lost his sense," they speculated. "Maybe he has come to his sense," the old men ventured. "Maybe he has decided to move his house to higher ground before the spring floods come."

As the days went on, the parts from the house began to take on another shape. It was unmistakable. A. Man was now building a raft. Carefully, piece by piece, the thing took shape. Noah? . . . An ark? . . . Could it be? . . . It couldn't be, or so said the preacher, for he had searched the scripture and assured the people that it could not be a second Noah: "Not water, but fire next time," he quoted the Bible.

"It *is* a sight on earth," the people said, when it seemed finished. But A. Man gave it hardly a second look. After chaining it to some nearby trees, A. Man disappeared from the community. Time passed and the children finally got up enough nerve to play on "The Ark," as it was being called. And, then, one fine spring day, looking up from spring planting, the people saw a great wagon lumbering into the community, complete with canvas top and spring seat, drawn by the finest team of matched mares as could be bought in Kentucky. Tied behind the wagon were a young brindle cow and a bull calf. Inside the wagon, hogs squealed and chickens cackled. Perched on the spring seat was A. Man. It was a noble thing, A. Man and his wagon, a thing designed to turn men's feet away from the soil and such mundane tasks as planting potatoes and cause them to strike out across a continent.

However, not for long was the wagon to lure people from the fields, for A. Man soon disassembled it and it, too, became a part of his raft. The raft now was finished. Wide Creek was standing at ten feet and rising. The raft tugged restlessly at the chains which held it. A. Man made a final trip into Wide

Creek and this time he had something to say: "I be leaving sometime tonight. I be needing a woman. If there be a woman hereabouts with sound body and sound mind to help—to be a helpmate—let her bring her things and come aboard tonight." This announcement had about the same effect in this Methodist community as if A. Man had announced a Saturday night dance. And, later, as A. Man's music, mixed with the sound of intermittent rain, filled the twilight hours, parents watched their daughters and not a few husbands worried about their young wives.

It was during the "Dinner on the Ground," which had to be held in the schoolhouse because of the rain, that Miss Sarah, the schoolteacher, first heard of A. Man's offer to take a woman with him. She heard it from the children. They had made a game of it. "A man wants a woman . . . A man wants a woman . . ." they chanted as they chased each other about the room on this last day of school. The children were to present a special program for their parents that afternoon, so Miss Sarah soon put a stop to that foolishness. Each year the

schoolchildren read selected literature aloud to their parents, designed to show their improvement in reading skills and assimilation of the proper community values. Earlier this year Miss Sarah had carefully selected new and different material in order to enliven the annual program with more interest, but when the preacher's precocious daughter began reading a selection Miss Sarah had been given by one of her professors at Normal School, the preacher objected. In the middle of her piece, he ordered his daughter to stop, looked at the papers from which she had been reading, and giving Miss Sarah a most austere glance said, "This is the work of Satan. I will not have my daughter reading such things." He then had his child read from the old reader, same as he had read when he was a child.

Miss Sarah suffered quietly through the rest of the afternoon as the program she had prepared so diligently was reduced by systematic parental objection to the old and familiar routine of years gone by. As the program came to an end and people began to leave, there were many who admonished Miss Sarah that she was young yet and perhaps didn't know that such literature was the workings of the devil and that she had best learn now that the old teachings were the best and true path to follow. Humiliated, Miss Sarah stayed behind, alone in her classroom and listened to the voices of the children as they were pulled along home by their parents. "A man wants . . . a man wants . . ." Miss Sarah had a way of turning everything around and looking at it from the other end: *A woman wants a man . . . A woman wants a man*— so became the chant in her head. It would not go away, but remained, lingering, like an old song and the quietly falling rain outside.

She came in the night, bringing little, knowing already that the raft was stacked high with provisions. Lingering a while on deck, she accustomed herself to the floating sensation. She listened to the stirring of the animals and the music coming from the wagon bed. *May as well be on with it*, she thought. Pushing aside the canvas flap she crept softly inside. A. Man stopped playing his music but said nothing.

"I heard you were looking for a woman," she said simply.

"Who be you and what can you do?" the man asked.

"I am the school teacher. I have brought clothes, maps, books about the Louisiana Purchase Territories, and other books and papers for teaching," she replied.

"How old you be?" the man asked.

"I am seventeen."

A long silence followed, while Sarah waited. She had come as far as she could. She had offered herself to him as a partner in whatever venture he had in mind. "You be very young." The pause continued. The decision was his. She was committed. "But it be good that *you* have come. I will treat you good—good as I treat myself." With that A. Man lay aside his fiddle and lay back on his bed.

"And I will be a good woman to you," Sarah said as she lay down beside him. In the night he wanted her and she was willing and A. Man took Sarah as his Woman.

Sarah's Diary

May 1, 1825—The debris is even worse today than it was yesterday. For a while we were caught up in a massive log jam. Much of the debris bares the unmistakable marks of man. The cut of the axe and saw, or the firescarred, half-burned trunks of massive trees cleared off of a thousand hillsides are all about me. I am beginning to feel a part of this— just another bit of driftwood cast afloat by some force greater than myself. But I know better. My being here is my own doing. A. M., as I call my man, doesn't talk much—always busy with something or playing the fiddle or banjo. I wish I knew more about A. M.

May 5, 1825—Again caught in a log jam most of morning. But it is an ill wind that blows no good. The log jam served as a bridge for a band of several scores of Indians to cross the river. Ahead of us not more than a few hundred yards a band of Indians, making a terrible wailing noise, men women and children, sometimes falling and crawling, pushed on by an angry group of soldiers and frontiersmen. There was another group of soldiers waiting on the other side who prodded the Indians on westward. I got the feeling at first that the Indians were just another bit of debris being swept seaward in nature's cleansing process—preparing a continent for new civilizations. But then as I watched women heavy with child crawling along the logs or saw scared children fished half-drowned from the cold water and old people carried in the arms of stronger braves I felt sorry for them. I couldn't help it. I know it is best to stick up for one's own kind. But sitting here on this raft, caught up in all this waste, I almost felt akin to all those Indians.

May 8, 1825—Still thinking about the Indians we saw yesterday. I tried to talk to A. M. about it. He only spit. I don't think I liked the way he spit. But he has been good enough to me. I guess that is what counts most. I decided to pray last night before I retired for the night. A. M. asked me what I was doing. I said I was praying. A. M. looked almost like he did when I tried to talk to him about the Indians. He didn't spit though. There is a lot I don't know about this man. But be that as it may. The die is cast and I have no regrets. I'll take my bitter with the sweet.

May 10, 1825—Rained all day today. Something different happened. We found a bear cub clinging for dear life to a log. A. M. pulled it aboard. It acts scared. But it is awfully cute. A. M. is trying to get it to suck the cow. Ole Brindle don't take too kindly to the idea. The other animals don't seem to relish the presence of a bear either.

May 15, 1825—The river is wider now—much wider. We are moving right along. Much warmer. We have seen several snakes the last few days. Another raft came alongside today. It was loaded with livestock and was being poled along by slaves. I had never seen slaves before. They were big black fellows, bare to the waist. A. M. exchanged talk with the owner of the raft. Sounds as if we are only a day or so away from the mouth of the Ohio River. It also sounded as if A. M. might be thinking about buying some slaves. He asked all about price, what kind were the best, who was a dependable trader and the likes of that. What have I gotten myself into?

May 17, 1825—We reached a place called Montgomery's Point today. It turns out that A. M. struck up some kind of a deal with the raft man he talked to a couple of days back. That man, his name is Elijah Smith, met us up-river with a boatload of his slaves and they came aboard our raft with long poles and helped land our raft. We are now tied up at a place called Egypt. I believe it is in a state called Illinois. I don't like this Elijah. I don't like the way he looks at me. All the white men are armed here with both knives and pistols. A. M. is wearing a knife and pistol. God knows he looks mean enough without them. There are several rafts tied up here. There are only a few women—mostly men. I called out to some of the women but haven't had a chance to talk to any of them yet. There is a big raft a hundred yards or so from ours. It seems to be a floating tavern of some sort. I can hear music and laughter from both men and women coming from there. There seems to be a lot of men coming and going all the time. I don't see any women coming and going but I can sure hear them over there. Cubby is growing and now takes everything for granted aboard our raft. A. M. is up to something. I'm sure of it.

May 19, 1825—Still tied up at Egypt. Place named right. Sure is no "Land of Canaan," that's for sure. Night before last A. M. went over to that raft where everyone—that is the men—are always coming and going. A. M. came back drunk as a skunk. I could hear fiddle and banjo playing. I'm sure it was A. M. playing the fiddle cause he came back and got his. I do know that I don't much like this place and will be glad when we move on. Then last night there was this dance on board the cattle raft right next to ours. They took the cattle off yesterday. A. M. and a couple of slaves did most all the playing for that dance. There was a bad fight and two men got cut up. But nobody bothered A. M. I believe that everyone, maybe including me, is afraid of A. M. There is a camp meeting going on here too. It is being held on shore under a brush arbor and they make most as much noise as the parties. The meetings last almost as late into the night too. I went over to the meetings and stayed for a while.

May 21, 1825—A strange man came aboard the raft today. I think he is a slave trader. I have left off praying for the time. This doesn't seem the proper place for it. Cub is up to a great deal of mischief. People seem almost as interested in him as they are in A. M.'s music. One of the mares had a fine stud colt this morning. A. M. was handy in helping the mare. That skill may come in handy later. I think I may be with child. I haven't told A. M. about it. I don't think it would make him any difference anyway.

May 23, 1825—What I thought would happen has happened. A. M. bought two slaves. They are the big strapping young fellows who played with him the other night. I think that is why A. M. bought them. Instead of some others. That slave trader paraded slaves by A. M. all day yesterday. The men felt of them and examined them just like they were horses. I am not sure I like this slavery business. Anyway, I wasn't asked about it. I guess that is men business, like going over to that drunken tavern.

May 25, 1825—There is lots of talk about the flooded condition of the Mississippi River. Worst ever, the old-timers say. Anyway we are on our way and I am glad. I wouldn't want to live in that Egypt place if they gave it to me. We are off to the promised land. A. M. and the two slaves, Pete and Jake, seem to know where the main river current is and have maneuvered the raft into it. How I don't know for there is water as far as I can see in every direction. I still take care of the animals and chickens and do the cooking. The slaves sleep out in the open under some canvas. A. M. and I still sleep in the wagon top. Mosquitoes are thick as clouds and constantly bite at us. The slaves don't seem to pay them any mind. When A. M. and the slaves aren't maneuvering the raft or working at something they often play on their musical instruments. All the streams coming into the Mississippi seem to be as flooded as the river itself. Sometimes I get the feeling that there isn't any place for all this water to go. I wonder if the ocean is getting full. Maybe that is silly thinking—but it is still raining a great deal.

May 29, 1825—Two additions to life aboard the raft. Something called a riverboat with a big paddle wheel and a steam engine came alongside our raft today. The riverboat was loaded with an assortment of slaves who were all chained together on the deck. The slave trader got in conversation with A. M. and convinced him that he needed to buy a couple of women for his two young slaves. I was surprised when A. M. went aboard the boat and began to examine the women slaves. A. M. examined the male slaves as if they were horses,

but he examined the female slaves as if they were cows. The more I see of this slave business the less I like it. Well A. M. picked out the best-looking pair of young females in the lot and bought them. They aren't more than fourteen or fifteen years old. A. M. seems to have an endless supply of gold.

June 2, 1825—Nature has taken her course. The slaves have already paired off. It was a thing that just happened. First there were glances from a distance, then there was encouragement, finally talk, then last night I heard them rutting together like animals, but they had paired off at different ends of the raft. Their coming together was not too unlike my coming to A.M. I guess I am constantly struck with how like us they are.

June 10, 1825—I'm having what some call morning sickness and Cubby has been causing all sorts of trouble—getting into everything. He has been prowling about at night getting into bed with everybody—getting most too big for his britches. He plays too rough with the calf and has broken into the chickens twice and keeps them in constant panic to where they have stopped laying eggs. I have the feeling that he is going to be bear stew before long if he doesn't watch out. But A. M. seems to enjoy his mischief.

June 13, 1825—A very strange thing happened today. An old bearded man in a dugout boat paddled out to our raft. God only knows where he came from. The old man was half wild and muttered a great deal as if he was talking to himself. He kept talking about an earthquake and steam and poison and vapors coming up out of the ground. He kept pointing westward and calling it *Hell*. It all had to do with something that had happened a good while back when even the Mississippi River had run backward. Now that the river was slowing down and was having trouble deciding which way it wanted to run the old man was afraid that all Hell was going to break

loose again. The strangest thing of all was how interested A. M. was in what this crazy old man was telling. A. M. got out maps and went over them with the old man. They talked a great deal about a "White River" which apparently mouthed somewhere down stream from where we now were. The old man had been all the way up the White River to where it bent west near the Missouri border. According to the old man the White River did not go through the area the old man described as Hell. The old man did not believe it would be possible to get a raft this size up the river—not very far anyway—not even if we had one of those steam engines.

June 16, 1825—The crazy old man is still with us—still babbling about his earthquake—which he says he witnessed. He has also been showing A. M. some items he has stowed away in his dugout. The items are apparently parts and pieces of a still. A. M. seems as interested in this as he was the slaves. My guess is that A. M. will keep the old man with us. The old man says that the distilling business is the noblest of work and that he knows as much about it as any man alive. He says he learned it from his dad who was a participant in the Whiskey Rebellion. The fact is, according to this wild old man, that is the reason he had left the east so he could ply his trade in peace away from government interference. I think that A. M. and the old man have something in common. The old man is running away from the government so he can make whiskey—A. M. is running away from the Methodists so he can fiddle. Anyway, I'd just as soon the old man had not come aboard with his knowledge of distilling whiskey, for I have been reading in the Bible about what happened to the first Noah after his bout with the flood. A. M. and the old man seem to be looking for some landmark. The slaves are working hard now with their long poles, testing the depth, pushing this way and that.

June 18, 1825—No question about it—we have left the Mississippi and are headed back north and west. Would you believe? The current is still with us. Some men came along yesterday. They were in a skiff of some sort. Said they were Slave Patrol. Told us we were on the White River. They explained the current going the wrong way by saying that there had been hurricane rains to the north and east and south, but that there had been no rains north and west so the Mississippi was filled up and backing up into its tributaries on the west. A. M. and the slaves have hoisted the sail and we are taking advantage of not only the mixed-up tide but also a southeasterly wind. A. M. is some sailor.

June 30, 1825 — It has been slow going now for days. The currents are mixed now. In the center of what must be the river channel the water is clear and trying to go down stream. Since I don't know where we are going I don't know how far we are from our destination. I asked A. M. about this and he said he would know it when we got there. We saw what looked like a plantation off to the east of us this morning.

July 4, 1825 — The wind has changed and is coming from straight ahead bringing an end to our float trip. The water is all clear and white now. I asked the old man if that was what gave the river its name. He didn't know but thought it had something to do with the fact that the White River was the boundary between Indian Territory and White Man's Land. The old man's name is Tauford Morrison.

July 6, 1825 — Old mother earth feels mighty good after all that time on board our raft. The colts and calf were happiest to get on land and spend a great deal of time kicking up their heels. The other mare had a colt a few days back. Seems late in the season for that. But no worse choice than I have made. I guess my first born will come in mid-winter. A. M. hitched the mares up today and tried to pull the raft upstream with chains from the bank. The thing was too much for them. The horses could not find good footing and the slaves were unable to keep the raft pushed far enough away from the bank.

I see Pinella being sick mornings like me. I guess it is no different with them. The Slave Patrol told us to watch our slaves and suggested that we get some dogs. But A. M. said that our slaves would be treated good and that maybe then they would not try to run away. They told A. M. he didn't know much about slaves. Tauford Morrison says the slaves are going to cause big trouble someday. He says that where we are going is not a good place for slaves anyway. Slaves belong in lowlands on plantations he says.

July 10, 1825 — A. M. has sent Pete and Tauford back down stream to offer to pay the plantation owner to bring wagons and help and try to haul our house and supplies farther upstream. This is a humid sickly place. Some Indians came downstream catching fish with their hands. A. M. watched them and learned how they did it. We now have fish to eat. Some Indian women were also beating buckbush roots on rocks in a creek back of where we are camped. Fish floated to the surface in the eddy and the children scooped them up with their hands. We are all busy reassembling things and sorting out supplies.

July 15, 1825 — Pete and the old man returned today. Tauford says that Mr. Brown, the plantation owner, said that he was sorry but he could not hire out any of his work force now during the growing season but would be willing to bring ten wagons to help out for about three weeks the last of August.

July 25, 1825 — A. M. and Pete have been gone nearly a week now. They have gone on upstream to search out a trail and find a suitable place to put our long-traveled house. I have been busy still sorting out supplies. It is hard to imagine all the things A. M. had stocked up with. Among other things

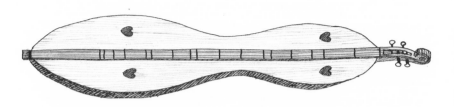

there is a complete blacksmith shop with enough metal to go into business. A. must have every woodworking tool there is. The sow had eight pigs. Good of her to wait until we were settled. I have setting hens in every tub and kettle I can spare. A. M. said it was better to go ahead and let the hens set seeing as how it would give the chicks time to grow up before cold weather. The old man is my protector. Cub has to be chained up most of the time now. Now that Old Brindle is getting all the grass she wants she is giving enough milk that we now have cheese and butter.

July 27, 1825—It has been an eventful day. Mr. Brown rode up to see about the business deal. He had several mean-looking, red-colored hounds with him. The dogs scared Cub so he broke his chain and has run away into the woods. But not before he had tore off one of the hound's ears. Mr. Brown looked over our stock of goods and the house and whistled. He wanted to know why we brought our house with us seeing as how there was plenty of timber where we were going to build a house. I told him we needed a raft to float all the other stuff on anyhow. I don't know if that is why A. M. did it this way or not. He said it looked to him like it would be cheaper just to build a new house. But I said I thought A. M. wanted to haul this house to our homesite. Mr. Brown said, "Well you meet one everyday." I said, "You sure do." Mr. Brown left the hound with the sore ear and told me to tell A. M. he would be back with *many* wagons the last week in August.

August 6, 1825—It has been an evil day. A family of people came down the river. The wife, heavy with child and already beginning labor, was tied to the dugout. The children sat in stunned silence and the man seemed beaten and dazed. Their name is Tollever and he said they had been living up north for nearly a year now and that the country had driven his wife mad. It was the loneliness mostly. That, plus hard work, sickness, fear from the Indians and outlaws. Tauford was most helpful. We put her in the wagon and tried to free her enough so she could have the baby. She screamed, kicked, bit and scratched and tried to get at the baby when it came. The slave girls helped and seemed to know about such things. They took the girl baby and cleaned it up and wrapped it. The baby seems to be all right. Tauford forced some wine he has been making from blackberries down the woman—most like drenching a cow.

August 7, 1825—A. M. returned last night. Seemed all excited for him. The woman is still demented. The husband wants to get on down river with her and the children. I haven't told A. M. yet but I'm thinking of keeping the baby. It would most likely die if they take it with them.

August 8, 1825—The family is gone. That is, all but the baby. I kept the baby. I guess it would be more accurate to say that the slave girls kept the baby. I do believe they wanted that baby. A. M. just as I expected didn't say one word. I don't believe anything bothers that man. The old man and A. M. are making big plans. The way they see it the people going west are likely to travel the high country rather than to get boughed down in the Arkansas mud of the lowlands to the south. Not only will the people travel across the uplands on the indian trails which abound, but many folks are likely to stay once they see the place—at least that is what A. M. believes. But I keep thinking about that woman gone mad and thinking about the ways of menfolk. We named the baby August.

August 18, 1825—A. M. and the two men slaves have been gone over a week. Have gone to blaze out a trail for the wagons and if they have time to put up some hay for the livestock come winter. Cub has not returned. The hound's ear is healing and she doesn't seem like such a ferocious beast after all. She follows me everywhere and gives me a sense of being safe. Altogether preferable to that stinking bear. There has been an abundance of wild fruit and greens. The slaves know about all sorts of plants and roots to eat. This place is bursting with life. The two slave girls are with child. I am with child. Chickens are hatching under a dozen setting hens.

August 21, 1825—A. M. and the slaves have returned. Mr. Brown and his string of wagons and mules are here. Mr. Brown is riding a big yellow Tennessee stud. One of the mares is in season so the men have been breeding her today. They chained a log up between two trees. They called it a teasepole. Then they held the mare and the stud on either side of the pole and let them bite and kick at each other for a time. Then after a while they let them come together. All the men were acting like little boys. Even the slaves all sat on one side and grinned. I guess men are all alike—women too, I suspect.

August 23, 1825—We are on our way again. We are a regular wagon-train. A. M. is walking ahead with Mr. Brown on the stud. Mr. Brown is a regular southern gentleman. Then there are the wagons pulled by the mules and then our wagon. Some things had to be left behind and will be gone back for later.

August 27, 1825—Suddenly the country has changed. There are rolling hills as far as one can see. Spring-fed crystal clear streams are everywhere. Trees and grass are in abundance. Game seems plentiful and there are few signs of people except an occasional group of Indians who hardly seem to notice us. Mr. Brown says the Indians will all be moved westward shortly. We have forded the river once and A. M. says we will ford it again. Sometimes on rough ground they double up the teams on the wagons.

September 5, 1825—It has been days now since we left the lowlands. Every day is a surprise now. I think I like these hills. Maybe because they are so much like the hills of home. I can just feel A. M. bursting with an anticipation of what he is going to do with this new country. I wonder if I will know the spot when I see it.

September 10, 1825—Well glory be! We are here! Even before A. M. halted the wagons I knew this was the spot. We are in a saddle between two of the highest hills around. There is a spring-fed creek running down off the mountain. The saddle slopes gradually down to where we forded the river. And could you believe that A. M. asked me where I wanted the house? I picked a spot on the west slope of the saddle above a waterfall and asked that it be faced toward the west with the creek and fall below. There is a large dry cave in the hillside just above the site.

September 12, 1825—Surprise! Surprise! I have a house! A. M. kept Mr. Brown and his slaves on and raised the house—complete roof and all in less than two days. A transformation has come over me. Finally I feel like something of A. M.'s is mine also. I find myself no longer like a girl but a woman giving orders to others, bossing the slaves around and once or twice I have made demands on A. M. It really surprised me when he hopped right to. He is now working Pete and Jake building a fireplace. Tillie and Pinella are daubing up the cracks in the cabin. Tauford is already building his still down by the waterfalls. I hope he doesn't get in the way of A's plans for a mill. Mr. Brown is supposed to return with two wagonloads of shelled corn. A. M. said he paid for that corn

with the last of his gold. So I guess that is the end of that mystery.

October 1, 1825—We are settled in. A. M. and the four slaves have been busy building lean-tos and outhouses for themselves, the chickens and the livestock.

October 28, 1825—Mr. Brown delivered the two loads of corn and brought us word that August's mother had made it as far as the plantation and died there. Mr. Brown believed that she had had hydrophobie because one of the children who she scratched had died also with similar symptoms. Mr. Tollever had taken the children and gone away but had returned to the plantation and was asking about the whereabouts of the baby. He had come back with a new 16-year-old bride. Mr. Brown said that there were quite a number of families wintering down at Arkansas Post who were planning on coming up in the Ozarks (that is the name of these hills) and homesteading come spring and that a goodly number of them were inquiring about the crazy man who had brought his house with him.

November 23, 1825—A. M. finally noticed my belly and patted it and said, "Looks like I be having a child." There is a great deal of activity. The clearing of land, splitting of rails, notching of logs, plowing for spring planting, caring for the livestock, cooking, housekeeping—very busy.

December 5, 1825—We had our first visitor since Mr. Brown. He was a very strange man. Said he was a Methodist missionary. A. M. brought the slaves into the house and they played dance music most all night. The missionary left bright and early the next morning. I wanted to ask the man to marry A. M. and me properly, but I was afraid to. I think A. M. intends to keep all preachers out of these hills with his music.

If A. M. doesn't keep them out with his fiddle, Tauford will with his still. The hound had six pups—all ears. Winter seems to be about the same here as back home.

December 25, 1825—Christmas Day! A. M. has been working all day in the woodshop. I got upset with him. Seemed to me like he could take off from his work at least on Christmas. I did suspect at one point that he might be making me something—a baby crib or something. So was I ever so surprised when he brought me a mountain dulcimer. I haven't seen one of those since my mother had one in Virginia. I have been strumming Christmas carols on it all evening. It is the right instrument for this country.

February 15, 1826—The baby came. I have to admit that I was a bit scared. But it was not really all that bad. I guess I will be able to have one every year. It is a boy and I named him Amus Man. They say I am to lie here in bed for the next 14 days. Horses and cows don't have to do that. A trader came by on a horse loaded down with all sorts of items. A. M. said he was a Jew. I had never seen a Jew before. He said that people were already talking about our place, calling it "Mansville." A. M. is silent on all these happenings, but I think he is secretly pleased. The building and clearing are coming along all right.

March 17, 1826—Spring has finally arrived. Along with it have come people. Five families have moved in hereabouts. Among the families is Mr. Tollever and his new bride. He is talking about taking August from us, but has not done so yet. The slave girls both have babies now. But we would still miss August. She is a very beautiful child and does not seem to be affected by her mother's madness. The cow has calved. She had a heifer this time. Last year's calf is a half-grown bull now and already feeling his oats.

April 1, 1826—Most of the newcomers are very poor. They continue to pour in on us. They are very dependent on us and come to us for everything. A. M. has been helping them, taking their word that they will help him out in return when they get on their feet. So we are busy, not only building our place, but also building a community. I think I am becoming a mid-wife. Me a granny woman at age 18! Mr. Tollever has been drinking too much of Tauford Morrison's brew. The Tollever family is living in the cave above our house and don't seem to be getting any crops in or preparing any permanent dwellings. I think we already have a town drunk. The new Mrs. Tollever is having a baby today so she must have been in some kind of trouble before they married. But who am I to talk. I am still not married.

April 15, 1826—A Mr. Huddle arrived at our place today with three wagons finely outfitted. He wants to put in a General Store and ferry down on the river below our house. He has been talking with A. M. A. M.'s only reservation is that Mr. Huddle is a devout Methodist. We have been having dances at each of the barn raisings, but I guess this is one where we won't. Mr. Huddle has very fancy womenfolk and I am not sure they approve of me since I go to the dances and have a man who plays the fiddle and allows a still on his place.

July 4, 1826—Just as A. M. suspected, Mr. Huddle has started up a revival meeting and is doing the preaching himself. But A. M. has offset that by letting Tollever and Tauford start a tavern next to the still.

September 15, 1826—One year has gone by. I can't believe what has happened here. There must be no less than fifty families hereabouts. There is a blacksmith shop, the beginnings of a mill with a water wheel, a still, a tavern, a woodshop—all belonging to A. M. There is a store and a church

and a ferry all belonging to the Huddles. Strangers come and go almost daily now, often frequenting the tavern. Mrs. Tollever spends a great deal of time at the tavern and seems to be a favorite of the customers. This Mrs. Tollever is sure not going to go mad from loneliness. Mr. Tollever is unconscious most of the time and Tauford is too crazy for anything. There is talk of a stave mill and handle factory going in. A. M. is thinking about putting in a cotton mill. And the menfolk have all pitched in and built a school down near the church. Guess who is the teacher? I'd have the first honest-to-goodness preacher who comes along to marry A. M. and me, but I can't have those fancy Huddle women knowing that their children's teacher is not properly married.

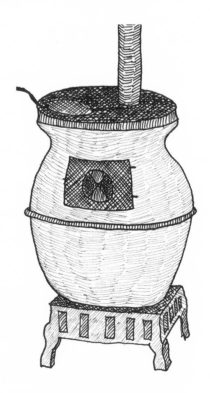

Oat Dees

OAT DEES HAD an unusual pet sow. The two were inseparable. Wherever Oat went the sow was sure to go. That wasn't usually a problem, since Oat didn't go to many places.

The two—Oat and Lula Bell, the Berkshire sow—lived out at the edge of the settlement, opposite the creek. So every day during the summer, just as regular as the mailman, Oat could be seen walking Lula Bell across the village to the creek beyond.

They could be seen first as they approached the crossroads by way of the path that cut diagonally across the weedy field surrounding the canning factory. They would come out into the road alongside the post office, cross over in front of the Methodist church and turn down a side road at Humberd's General Mercantile Store, passing the spit-and-whittle club sitting on the front porch. Uncle Abe, the unofficial chairman of the spit-and-whittle club, would always take out his watch as Oat and Lula Bell passed, just as he did when the Star Route mailman came by. Abe was the local timekeeper of events. "Hum-m-m, running a little slow today."

Lula Bell might stop for a spell, specially on hot days and watch the men pitch horseshoes out back of the store in the shade. Of course, if she stopped, Oat would too. After a while Oat and the sow would take another path alongside Kelley's Blacksmith Shop and disappear over the bank of the creek.

For two hours Lula Bell would wallow in the cool mud of the stream while Oat sat on the bank scratching her with a long stick. When Lula Bell got ready to leave she would splash around in the creek and wash off the mud. Then they would start back home, Lula Bell leading the way. Occasionally the man and the sow might stop at the store for some salt or other human essential, but this was rarely the case.

Uncle Abe would again check the time as they came back by the store, just as he had when Oat and Lula Bell had passed going down to the creek. Uncle Abe would usually speak; the other men might look up from whittling and nod. Lula Bell might grunt if she felt like it, and Oat would usually look away.

On one of those rare occasions when Oat and Lula Bell stopped at the store, Uncle Abe tried to strike up a conversation with Oat while Lula Bell went about sniffing the neat piles of shavings at the feet of the men sitting on nail kegs and tomato crates.

"Seems like a awful waste of time a-goin' down to the creek and staying all that time every day . . ." Abe said.

Lula Bell seemed to ignore the remark, but Oat stopped and thought—or seemed to—for some time before he surprised everyone by making one of the longest speeches anyone had ever heard him make.

"Well . . ." he said, "yes, but I don't 'spect time means much to a hog . . ."

W. C. Corey, 83

94

Mad Dog

A POWERFUL DOG, something of a mixture between a redbone hound and a bloodhound, lay under his master's porch. From time to time a shiver would run the length of his body, seeming to start somewhere in his brain and ending with a twitching of the tail. Occasionally the dog would whine low and try to get up, bumping his head against the porch.

"You seed Old Red today?" Cora Blalock asked her husband as she swatted another fly.

"Naw, but I hear him down under the porch fussing at the flies. I guess he's ashamed of that smell of skunk on him. He ain't much for coming around during hot spells," Lester Blalock answered as he looked wistfully out toward the barn. A mournful bellowing came from the barnlot where dust could be seen rising from the sick cow chained to the big oak.

"That cow is mad, I tell you Lester, and you'd best shoot her and get it over with," Cora asserted.

"They's likely lots of things that would make a cow act like that. I'm a-gonna wait a little longer and see if she don't get better," Lester countered.

"There ain't nothing that makes a cow act like that that she gets well from. Nothing! You're just too soft-hearted to kill anything 'cepting squirrel and rabbits. You was the same way when that old white horse broke his leg. You let him lay around and suffer for days before you finally shot him," Cora accused.

There was a series of thumpings under the house as Old Red, bumping each floor joist, crawled out from under it. The dog stood in the yard and faced up toward his master on the porch. His eyes seemed to be glazed over. He stood uncertainly on his legs, his tail drooping, a greenish froth dripping from his mouth.

"What's the matter, Red? Get a little hot for you under there?" Lester asked. "Think by now he'd learned to duck his head when he comes out from under there."

"As a general rule he don't bump his head," Cora said. "They's something wrong with that dog too. Just you wait and see. If you was a-doing what you ought, you'd shoot that dog right now."

"You always been against my hunting so you ain't never liked my dogs," Lester said as he got up to go down and take a closer look at Old Red.

Red faced his master unsteadily and, for the briefest moment, seemed almost to recognize him. But as Lester approached, the dog turned aside and trotted slowly toward the front gate.

"Here, Red!" Lester called.

The dog did not stop, but bumped into one of the gate posts, backed up, and then ran into the other post before making its way through the gate towards the wood lot.

As a crow flies, it is ten miles from Lester Blalock's to the Pine Grove community. The hound was traveling in a straight line when Winerfred Gray first saw it. It seemed reluctant to go around anything and bumped into several things that were in its way. Each time it bumped into something it would snap out with its teeth, slobbering all the time.

"I guess I could of shot it easy as not," Winerfred said later, "but you don't just go around shooting a fine-looking hound like that, 'specially when it's got on a collar and all."

As the hound passed by Winerfred's place, his three dogs came out and gave chase, all jumping on the hapless creature before they could stop themselves. The strange dog didn't really fight off his dogs, Winerfred later recalled, but simply nipped at them from side to side as he went on his way, pulling the other dogs along. After only a brief contact, Winerfred's dogs, seeming to sense something wrong, gave up the struggle and returned to their front porch, whining, their tails between their legs.

"They looked and acted like they had been caught sucking eggs," Winerfred said. "I guess the word mad dog came to me but I didn't ever quite say it."

The second person to see the dog was Mr. Fredman, the mailman. "He was standing right on top of the bank as I came across that low-water bridge down there on Honey Creek. I guess he was standing there on account of the water in the creek 'cause I've heard tell that mad dogs don't like water. 'Course I didn't have no way of knowing that he was mad at the time. If I'd knowed it I would of just run over him. Could of done it easy. Instead, I got out and went over and took a hold of his collar to see if there was some kind of tag on it. Just had a tag that said, 'Carroll County Coon Hunting Association, Box 48, Berryville, Arkansas.' When I turned him loose he just sorta snapped at me as if he was snapping at a fly. Didn't touch me or nothing. Just went on down the road ditch bumping into things and snapping at them. I kind of wondered if he might be mad but I don't guess I'd of thought any more about it 'cepting when I got around to Winerfred Gray's place he was waiting for me and he got to telling me about a dog that had come through his place earlier and it sounded like that same dog so we got to wondering out loud if it wasn't maybe mad. So I started telling peo-

ple along the route to watch out for a dog that was acting kind of strange but I didn't tell nobody it was mad, 'cause I didn't know for a fact if it was mad. They'd just have to come to their own way of thinking about that when they seed it.''

Mr. Fredman had already passed the schoolhouse before he saw the dog, so no one had told the school about the strange dog.

The teacher, Mr. Bates, didn't think much about it when he first looked out during the noon hour and saw a dog standing in the school yard. He remembered he did think the dog looked like it had been running hard and was tired and had maybe got lost on some all-night fox hunt. The children weren't paying any attention to it and it didn't seem to be bothering anybody so Mr. Bates just left it alone at first. A little while later, he looked out and saw some of the smaller children trying to feed the dog some leftover lunch. He thought it was strange the dog was not eating the food. Then a strange sensation went through him and the words ''mad dog'' began to form on his lips.

''My first instinct,'' Mr. Bates testified later at a Board of Directors' meeting, ''was to cry out a warning, *mad dog!* But I figured it would frighten the children causing them to panic in all directions. So I decided to go to the hallway and ring the bell. It wasn't quite time for the bell but maybe none of the children would suspect anything. So I began ringing the bell. Luckily the children all began moving toward the schoolhouse like usual. But so did the dog. I remembered then that I had heard somewhere that mad dogs were attracted to sound. I became terrified. It was like a nightmare. They all seemed to be moving toward me together—the dog and the children. I didn't know what to do so I stopped ringing the bell. I usually keep ringing until they are all in the schoolhouse. Since there were children behind the dog and there were children in front of the dog, I did the first thing that came to my mind. I closed the door on the girls' side and stood in the boys' side and called out as loud as I could, 'the last one in eats dirt!' I shouted it over again and again as I motioned the children in the one door. The dog was coming also, but not so fast as the children now. Everyone except Teddy Collins made it to the door before the dog. The dog was just ahead of Teddy so I had to slam the door on both of them. The dog bumped into the closed door and then swerved and started back down the steps. But just as it did that it brushed against Teddy, coming up, and reached out and nipped him on the ear. Then I let Teddy in and started ringing the bell again so everyone would know that there was something wrong at the school. Of course, you know the rest of what happened."

The ringing of the school bell alerted the Pine Grove community that something was amiss up at the grammar school. Since many people had already heard of the possibility that there might be a mad dog on the loose they were fearful that the dog had gone to the school. Their worst fears were proven true when they all gathered in the school yard and word passed from person to person, "There's a mad dog loose and it's done been here and bit the little Collins boy."

Sam Blevins, who was the chairman of the Board of Directors of the school, and thus the highest-ranking elected official in the community, took over the meeting at the school house.

"The first thing we got to do is to get a mad stone for Teddy," Mr. Blevins announced.

"That's not going to do any good—" said the teacher, "what that boy needs is a doctor."

"I ain't against doctors when they is needed," said Mr. Blevins, "but what we need now is a mad stone. Does anybody know where there's a mad stone?"

Several people had heard of a mad stone over in Eureka Springs that had worked on other people. Mr. Fredman said that since he had the only car in the community he would be glad to take young Collins to Eureka Springs to the mad stone. He was quite sure he could be back by nightfall.

"That'll be soon enough," Mr. Blevins assured everybody. "If we get that boy to that mad stone and it sticks to the boy's ear we'll know it took and that boy'll be out of the woods. What we need to do now is to get these children all home without anybody else getting bit and put up our livestock and then hunt down this mad dog and kill it."

The people all agreed that the best way to get the children home was to find enough wagons to haul them and to have an armed man accompanying each wagon.

While they were still discussing how they might best hunt down the mad dog, Lawrence Lane rode up on a horse and announced that he had already killed the dog over near the store. It had been coming at him right down the middle of the road when he shot it. Winerfred Gray asked Lawrence to describe the dog.

"It was a big shepherd dog," Lawrence explained.

"That's not the mad dog—" Winerfred said, "fact is, it sounds like *my* dog."

"Don't matter none whether it is or it ain't," Sam Blevins said. "We're going to have to kill all our dogs that ain't been put up long as this is going on."

"Don't make no sense going around a-killing dogs that ain't mad," Winerfred retorted, getting quite riled up.

"Don't matter none. You'd have to kill him anyway if he's been loose," Sam repeated and most everyone agreed. Winerfred cast his troubled eyes toward town.

By the time the children were all gotten home and the livestock secured, darkness had settled over the community. Some of the menfolk had gathered up at the Collins' place to wait for Mr. Fredman to return with the boy. They could hear the Ford coming up the hollow for a couple of miles before they could see its lights.

"It worked," Mr. Fredman announced as he climbed out of his machine and brought the boy up onto the porch and into the glow of a kerosene lamp. "The mad stone belonged to that old Indian, Mr. Gott, over in Eureka. He says he got it out of a stomach of a all-white deer. They say it's a ball of hair that has done turned to stone.

"Well, anyhow, I took the boy to that old Indian and we

laid him out there on the ground and Mr. Gott he went to soaking that mad stone in some fresh warm milk from a fresh cow. Then he lays that stone on that cut on Teddy's ear. Well it lays there a spell and then the old Indian tries to pull it off and they is stuck together tight as you please. So he leaves it on a spell longer so as to draw out all that poison.''

Most people felt better about the boy, but the teacher told them that he had read about a scientist who had found a cure for rabies and that a good doctor would know about such things. But the Collinses and most of the others were pleased with the treatment and spoke of similar cases where the mad stone had worked.

Night settled over Pine Grove. Here and there dogs would set to barking and a frightened farmer would go to his cabin door and look out into the night. There seemed to be more barking of dogs than usual. The barking seemed to travel around the country from farm to farm. First one bunch of dogs and then another would set up a mournful howling as if they sensed the calamity that had come upon them. Occasionally, a shot or two would ring out as one farmer or another fired at something moving in the bushes.

When morning came, it was a day like any other hot summer morning, except that the people all ventured from their homes carrying either a gun or a club or a pitchfork—something to fight off the mad dog should they come upon him suddenly. Men gathered early at the school to plan the day's hunt and compare stories on what had happened during the night. If the dog had been in a small fraction of the places people were sure he had been, he was one busy dog. If the dog had escaped harm from the great volleys of shots aimed at him by men who could shoot the eye out of a squirrel at a hundred yards, he was one lucky dog.

The dog could be any place. He could be in the next clump of bushes. He could be under the porch, the house, in the haybarn, the road ditch, or under the next culvert. Or he could be gone altogether or maybe dead. Another problem was that there were some dogs in the community which looked something like Old Red and most dogs were beginning to act strange, what with people running all over the countryside with guns and clubs.

By mid-morning there had been two authentic reports of the dog. As if to add insult to injury, the dog showed up at the Collins place. Mrs. Collins heard a commotion down near the chicken house. She grabbed up a soap paddle from the black kettle in the backyard and went down to see what was bothering the chickens. When she saw the dog it was already between her and the house. The menfolk were all gone looking for the dog but the children were watching from the porch. They began to scream at their mother when they saw her going toward the chicken house door. The children remembered something that she in her fear of the moment had forgotten. Lately, someone had been stealing the Collins's chickens and so Mr. Collins had rigged up a shotgun which he had loaded and cocked and mounted back in the hen house pointed right at that door. There was a cord tied to the door and strung up over a joist and back to the trigger of the gun.

The blast cut Mrs. Collins almost in two, killing her instantly.

"I should of knowed it," Mr. Collins said when he got there. "Trouble always comes in threes. I wonder what will be next?"

"One possible trouble could be avoided maybe if you would get a doctor for that boy," the teacher said.

"What's gonna be's gonna be," the old man reflected.

Some of the women of the community came in to lay out Mrs. Collins. They patched her up as best they could, washed her, closed up the wounds and body openings with cloth, draped her Sunday clothes over her as best possible, combed her hair and balled it back, tied a dish rag around her head and under her chin, put a copper penny on each eye, stretched her out on a buntling board awaiting the coffin.

The men divided themselves into three groups. A small group went down to the blacksmith shop to make a cedar box

107

for the burying. Another group went up to the graveyard and began digging the grave. The remaining men continued to hunt for the dog.

Brother Ashby went down in the Collins pasture, down on the pond bank to pray. "God in Heaven, these is dog days," he reminded the Lord. "... days when even snakes is blind as they sheds they skins, days when waters are troubled and muddied as they turns over, days when big fish lay back in they holes and are afraid of neither man nor beast, days when wounds won't hardly heal, days when dogs goes mad . . ."

It was then that Brother Ashby heard the peculiar noise in the heavens. It was a sound which he had heard before. Come to think of it, it was that very sound which had changed his life, causing him to become a preacher. The first time he had heard that sound was when he was a mere lad. He had been a barefoot bashful boy on his way to observe a brush arbor revival where on previous nights he had hid among the trees and watched the foot-washings, the shouting, the praying, singing and preaching. But as he made his way across the countryside on that night years ago he had heard a bell in the heavens, just like the one he now heard. On that occasion, so many years ago now, he had taken the sounding of the bell as a sign from God—a call to preach! Rushing in to the meeting, he had fallen there before his God and given his life to Christ. He had gotten up from that tear-stained altar a new man and had gone back to his old mother's cabin down on Indian Creek and announced, "Don't get scared Ma, I'm gonna pray!" And from that day to this he had not only prayed, but he had stirred and moved hundreds to Christ with his preaching, telling always of the bell he had heard in the heavens and calling out to people all over the Ozarks and elsewhere, "Don't get scared Ma, I'm gonna pray!" But that was all in the distant past and it was the present which Brother Ashby now had to face. . . .

So he opened his eyes, looking expectantly toward heaven for the sign he needed on this troubled day. There was something hovering over him, not more than fifty feet away. "It is like one of them winged creatures out of the Bible," the preacher cried, trying desperately to maintain his faith. Doubt flooded his very soul, as he continued to focus his eyes on the creature. His very call to preach the gospel was being brought into question by what he saw. It was a trick of the devil. It *was* the devil! He would cast it out, exorcise it. The preacher scrinched his eyes closed and rebuked the repulsive creature: "In the name of the Father, the Son, and the Holy Ghost I cast thee from me," he commanded. "Thou foul demon on wings of an earthly buzzard, be gone. Be removed from me as far as the East is from the West!"

Mustering all his faith, believing with all his heart, certain that the awful creature would be lying dead at his feet, the preacher opened his eyes and looked about. The creature had changed its form. It no longer had the wings of a buzzard and was no longer airborne. A four-footed red demon took shape before his very eyes, chasing its tail, circle upon circle, faster

and faster, a green froth dripping from an extended bloody tongue.

The preacher stood up, transfixed, as these images changed before his very eyes. Demons seemed to hover all about, amidst a beating of wings and ringing of bells. The preacher knew enough about demon possession to realize that he must keep his mind on the Lord or there was a good chance that he would become possessed himself.

The big red four-footed demon now lay at his feet, twitching and jerking, while the winged demons hovered about. Some alighted nearby. Gradually the red demon became a dog, a big red hound—the *mad dog*! The preacher's faith faltered and he fell backwards into the pond.

At just about that moment, Old Red recovered his balance and staggered off across the field and the buzzards again ascended into the heavens to hover over the dying dog. The wet and troubled preacher struggled out of the pond and walked up to the graveyard to tell the men what had happened. The men in the grave stopped their digging and leaned on shovels and picks. The men up top rested on the relatively cool mound of fresh dirt as they heard Brother Ashby's troubled tale.

Suddenly, as if in confirmation of Brother Ashby's story, they all became aware of a bell ringing. Looking up, they saw the buzzard. Just as suddenly, seeming to know what to expect next, they saw the dog. He had stumbled to the edge of the grave, swaying back and forth, clumsily deciding whether to try crossing over it or go around. Two men were down in the grave and the other three men, including the preacher, were across the grave from the dog. The guns were all leaning against a tree near the dog, out of reach.

The preacher fell down straightway before his God and begged for deliverance from this evil thing. The only answer he got was a gun sounding somewhere in the distance and another dog yelping in death.

One of the gravediggers took up a shovel and was slipping around the end of the grave toward the mad dog. The only sound that could be heard now was the heavy breathing of Old Red. A buzzard was again overhead. The gravedigger came down hard on the back of Old Red's head. The dog fell down like he had been dropped with a bullet. Then he began to quiver and kick around in a circle on his side, finally falling over the bank into the nearly-finished grave with the two men inside.

Old Red was still burning on a brush pile down the hill a piece as people began gathering at the schoolhouse for the Collins funeral. The buzzards continued to circle over the area as the congregation sang,

"Oh they tell me of a home
Far beyond the skies
Oh they tell me of a home
Far away . . .

"Oh they tell me of a home
Where no storm clouds rise
Oh they tell me
Of an unclouded day . . ."

A subdued Brother Ashby spoke of a God who sometimes spoke to people through dumb animals in mysterious ways, warning them of the wrath to come. Then the preacher talked for a short while about a New Heaven and a New Earth and a bright day coming, just like the song says. The people marched by and showed their respect and whispered about how natural and at peace Sister Collins looked. "Just like she was asleep." Then the people followed the body to the graveside where Brother Ashby sprinkled dust on the casket and said, "Dust thou art and to dust thou shalt return." And then the people all went home to look for madness in *their* dogs and wait and worry.

The Collins children now had two games to play. The empty corncrib lent itself very well to both games. Playing church had long been a favorite pastime. They would get inside the corncrib and pretend they were grownups—singing, shouting, washing feet, testifying, preaching and praying. Recently they had been playing a new game called "Mad Dog." They would all get in the corncrib and one of them would go mad and act like a dog slashing out at everyone. Then the others would try to rush out the door and fasten the door on the one inside who was acting mad.

Exactly two weeks after Teddy Collins had been bitten by the mad dog the Collins children were all down in the corncrib playing church. Teddy was playing Brother Ashby and had already told about hearing the bell and had just said, "Don't get scared Ma, I'm gonna pray," when suddenly he stopped, grabbed his head and throat and fell down on the floor and began to thrash about. After a while he got up on his hands and knees and began looking about queerly, eyes glazed. He began to chew his tongue. Blood and saliva dripped from his chin.

The other children immediately changed games, from "church" to "mad dog," and quickly scrambled out of the building, locking the door behind them. But this was not the way the game was supposed to be played. They had never gone directly from one game to another before. Furthermore, no one had ever chewed his tongue until it bled before. So the other children watched Teddy through the cracks in the corncrib to see what he was going to do next. Teddy continued chewing his tongue there on all fours. The children tried pushing sticks through the cracks of the crib, teasing him as they had before to get him to bite at them, but they got no response, just glazed, vacant stares. Finally, they left Teddy in the crib and went down in the field to tell their dad.

"Teddy's been playing mad dog, and he won't stop so we left him locked up in the corncrib!" they told their father.

"I thought I told you children to stop playing that mad dog game," the tired and worried man said as he looked toward the corncrib.

As they went on to the end of the field where Mr. Collins could tie up his mules they noticed that the teacher, Mr. Bates, had gotten off his horse in front of the house. Mr. Bates had called on the Collins most every day lately.

"Where is Teddy?" Mr. Bates asked as they approached him.

"We was playing church and then Teddy started to playing mad dog and then he wouldn't quit so we left him locked up in the crib and went to get dad," Thersia explained.

The men looked at each other, neither saying a word as they approached the crib. They could see Teddy through the cracks. He was on his feet now, walking about in a circle amongst the corn shucks.

"Teddy, what are you doing in there?" the father asked as he started to unlatch the door.

"Don't unlock that door!" the teacher shouted from where he was standing.

"Why not?" the father asked.

"Come here and look!" the teacher answered.

They were all peeking at Teddy through the cracks. Except for the fact that he was now standing, he was just as he had been when the children had left to get their father. He stood there, totally oblivious to their presence, eyes dilated and glazed, blood and saliva oozing from his mouth.

"The boy is mad," the teacher said.

The father started to unbar the door. The teacher stood in his way and said, "No! He must stay locked in there. We will fix it as comfortable for him as we can."

Teddy Collins lived in hell for the next nine days. He did not eat or drink or sleep. People gathered as word spread of his madness and there were always some folks at the corncrib until it was over, watching, waiting.

"It is hard to get a mad stone to stick good to something like your ear," they said.

The Ice Cream Supper

I'VE BEEN TRYING TO REMEMBER the year of the big freeze. I think it was the same year they started those big wars in Europe. I remember it that way 'cause I recollect hearing some of the old men down at the store trying to explain the big freeze. They said it had something to do with the wars, the shooting of all them big guns and that sort of thing. They said it always happens like that in times of wars—all sorts of freakish weather. The men said that it had been like that during the last great war and they had heard tell that it was that way during the War Between the States.

Well, I don't know about that sort of thing but the men seemed to think that whoever it was that caused the weather—God or the devil, depending on the kind of weather—sometimes heard them big guns and got mixed up thinking it was thunder and got the idea he should turn it colder. As I said, I don't know about that but I do know we had a big freeze and that was almost our undoing. . . .

It was the winter after we had had that rousing revival where Uncle Joe Gott had been converted from a Fire Baptized Holiness to a Free Pentecostal Holiness. How I remember that is 'cause I was thinking about the big baptizing while we were cutting the ice off the river that winter. You see, the Fire Baptized Holiness hadn't believed in water baptism so when Uncle Joe got the Holy Ghost and was converted to Free Pentecost he wanted to be baptized in the worst way. So when Brother Adams took that long line of summer converts down to the river singing:

"Shall we gather at the river
  The beautiful, beautiful river . . ."

Uncle Joe was leading the host despite his 103 years (for the twenty years I knew Uncle Joe he was always 103 years old). Anyway, when Brother Adams stopped singing and lifted his hands to say, "Uncle Joe, in the name of the Father, the Son and the Holy Ghost, I now baptize thee," Uncle Joe cried out so all the Fire Baptized Holiness within a mile could hear,

"Hold me under till I blubber!" I don't know if Uncle Joe blubbered or not but he did come up a-shouting and a-splashing water all over the place and mighty nigh drowned Brother Adams. Turns out there were those in the community who wished he had drowned Brother Adams after Brother Adams got into trouble with that girl over at Holcomb.

But I didn't want to talk about that, although it is hard not to think about Uncle Joe once you get started thinking about him. (Last time I was in Eureka Springs I got to thinking about Uncle Joe Gott and the time we were going to the camp meeting down at White Oak, and we were all riding in the back of Larry Lane's old Model A truck. Uncle Joe got happy and started shouting and praising God just like he was at church just from looking at them fine houses along the road, sort of built on top of each other. It was most too much for the old Indian. He got so carried away that we were afraid he was going to fall off the truck and hurt himself, or be caught up to heaven in a chariot or something. This all happened a long time before Gerald K. Smith put the big cross up on the hill and began the passion plays reminding all the people how it was the Jews that killed Jesus.)

The thing I remember about that winter is how cold it was when we either walked or rode in a wagon to church. You see, the good feeling generated by the big revival lasted right on into the winter. So we went to church all the time. I remember one night I was walking to church and there was an awful cold frost sparkling everywhere and I saw this object shining in the snow and I thought it was maybe an expensive ring like the women was always discarding when they got Sanctified at the meetings. So I reached down to pick it up and came up with a big gob of Uncle Joe's spit that he had just relieved himself of.

Well, that night I was thinking about Uncle Joe Gott, we got right out on the ice with the saws and we sawed the ice up in big slabs and then we took a horse that Jim Wilnot had put special ice shoes on that had real sharp spikes and we hauled the ice on sleds and put it in the basement of the old Jordon place. Then we got wagonloads of sawdust from Bailey's sawmill and packed the ice in that and waited for summer. At the time nobody could see anything wrong with it. It seemed perfectly innocent.

That seems strange when you look back at it, for we knew all along that we were going to make ice cream come summer —that is, providing the ice didn't melt in the meantime. And if we had thought about it at all we would have realized that we might be making the ice cream as a group since the ice belonged to everybody. But not even Sister Lane or Brother Wilnot who usually looked out for our spiritual welfare and guarded us against the wiles of Satan were alert to what we were about to get ourselves into.

You don't have to believe this unless you want to, but that ice lasted most all summer. The summer started off as innocent as you please. When anybody wanted ice they would just go get it. Since the ice had come from the beautiful, beautiful river, it wasn't clean enough to use for nothing except making ice cream and the likes of that. All in all, it was a good spring and early summer—what with the war going on, farm prices going up. There was more work for everybody, people were talking about a five-dollar day, and the big guns or something were bringing plenty of rain. Hence there was plenty of milk and hence plenty of ice cream.

Come to think about it, it was just exactly the sort of season that you would expect people to become lax and forget about Jesus and start having get-togethers not centered around having church. That is just what happened. Some one suggested why didn't they all just bring their freezers and ingredients over to the Jordon cellar and all make ice cream together? So once a week, at first, on a non-church night, the people all began to meet to make ice cream. Right off you got the makings of something evil—the potential for Satan to come among the people. Anybody knows that there are a lot of things that can happen at an ice cream supper besides just making ice cream and eating it and getting a headache. It doesn't matter if you do call it an ice cream supper instead of an ice cream social. A social by any other name is still a social.

First off, you got the possibility that there is going to be gossip, specially by the womenfolks. Then there is going to be competition. The women are going to compete over who can make the best batch of ice cream. The men are going to compete over nearly everything, like who can crush the ice the best by swinging the broadside of an axe against a chunk of ice held in a gunnysack or who can crank the freezer the best or who can get the right mixture of ice and salt or who gets the worst headache. The children are going to compete over who gets to lick the paddle or who gets to sit on the freezer to hold it down while the men crank it over.

It's awful easy for people to get too friendly at ice cream suppers. A man bragging on some women's batch of ice cream or a woman being complimentary about how hard a man has frozen a batch of ice cream can have all kinds of different meanings. People can bump into each other in the dark and it may not be accidental at all. This happens all the time and it's exactly the sort of thing the devil is just waiting for.

You have to also consider the influence such events have on the children. You got sort of a soft summer evening with adults busy with freezing ice cream and therefore not too attentive. You have children, boys and girls, out in the dusk playing hide and seek or chasing fireflies. Just look at the loose way the young people are handled at your usual ice cream supper! There is hardly any praying or singing or any form of planned activity. Anybody knows that an idle mind is the devil's workshop and you got a lot of idle minds at your average ice cream supper.

You got to admit that the devil is a sly one. He began coming at us in all them ways. Here we was having church regular and a-shouting and singing most every service with people getting saved right along, some of them for the second or third time, and then we start them ice cream suppers.

Just as you'd guess, the women got to gossiping right off. They gossiped about different ones but mainly about the

preacher's wife, Sister Adams. They said she was lazy, not very clean, didn't keep a good house, hung out terrible-looking washes on Monday, was sick all the time, and they was most afraid to eat her ice cream the way she cared for her milk.

Well, a thing like that was bound to get back to Brother Adams. 'Course he knew it was the truth. But that didn't matter—he still didn't like it. So he preaches a sermon about gossipy women and that didn't set too well with most, so there wasn't much shouting about that.

Then some of the women got hurt because no one ever seemed to brag on their ice cream. They felt that they would just as leave not come if it was going to be that way. So some of them did say they was sick and stayed home but their husbands kept coming and that was as good as the devil wanted.

It all sort of come to a head when late that summer Sister McKinney finally told her husband that Brother Lester had pinched her. And Brother McKinney in turn told Brother Wilnot who in turn told Brother Adams. They had a church meeting where they "churched" Brother Lester and Sister McKinney. And there was some things came out at that church trial that shouldn't happen to anybody. It happens

that pinching Sister McKinney wasn't all that Brother Lester had done.

It seems it had all started with the ice cream suppers way back in the early summer. The Lesters and the McKinneys had taken to riding to the suppers together in Brother Mc-Kinney's truck, with all of them riding in the cab. They sometimes sang as a quartet at church so they would practice on the way to the suppers. They would be coming down the road singing, "Just a Little Talk with Jesus," and get happy and start shouting and praising the Lord and Brother Lester would say, "Now everybody keep your mind on the Lord." But at that church meeting they made Brother Lester tell what he was doing while everyone else was supposed to have their minds on the Lord.

Well, everybody at the church meeting got all worked up. It most likely would have gone on forever if Brother Lester hadn't of confessed outright and gotten saved again for the fifth time. Brother Adams preached a powerful sermon that showed everybody the evils of meeting together for anything 'cept the worship of the Lord.

There weren't no more ice cream suppers that summer. Couldn't of gone on much longer anyhow. The ice from the big freeze had finally thawed.

Marble-Playing in the Ozarks

IF YOU GO TO THE OZARKS these days you aren't likely to find grown men, out back of crossroad stores, playing marbles. But you will find, if you look closely, many grown men, middle-aged or older, with an extra-large thumb. That great thumb may tell a story. It may tell a story of a great champion—a champion as skilled as any athlete, in any sport, at any time, in any place.

So far as I know no one has ever immortalized one of these great champions. No magazine has ever carried his picture. There have been no feature articles heralding forth with every little detail of some great marble player's personal life. None was ever interviewed on the five o'clock news. There is no hall of fame for great marble players!

In fact, it is extremely doubtful if you can now find, in all these United States of America, one smooth, level, hard, marble playing ground. Such areas have long since grown up in weeds or been replaced by a poolroom, domino parlor, or even horseshoe pits. Not even Blue Eye, Missouri, still hosts a single marble game. All you will find is a few old men with big thumbs. And even these old men can hardly recall the ground rules of the game. In my travels in the Ozarks, I was unable to find one complete set of nine stone marbles. And choice agate taw marbles are now considered antiques. This all seems more the pity when one reflects a bit on the game of marbles. It would be difficult, indeed, to invent a more innocent, more wholesome, less expensive, potentially universal, or physically more challenging recreational sport than marbles.

The game of marbles is so devoid of corruption that I have never talked to anyone who has ever heard of a single instance of betting on the game. About the most wicked thing that might happen at a marble game is that someone might *fudge*. Of course I'm not talking about the game of "keeps," that schoolchildren play. That game is played in a round circle and is frowned on by strict teachers as a corrupting practice. So of course you will still find children playing keeps. Maybe the real game of marbles died out because it had so little of the element of sinning in it, that it just wasn't that much fun! If it had been outlawed, no doubt it would still be flourishing.

In any case, the game of marbles is played on a six-foot square drawn out on hard smooth ground. Nine stone marbles, usually brought to the game in an old tobacco sack, are used for playing. In addition, each player brings to the game his favorite agate taw marble for shooting. One of the stone marbles is placed in the center of the square. This marble is called the "center man." Four of the stone marbles are placed at each of the four corners of the square and are called "corner men." The remaining four marbles are placed on the outside lines of the square midway between the corner marbles. These marbles are called "line men." Another six-foot line is drawn parallel to one side of the square four feet away. It is from this line that each player in turn must begin his shooting.

The game may be played with singles or doubles. That is, two men may play against each other or two pairs of men may play against each other. In either case, the players shoot in turn. The player who is to shoot first is determined by standing back of the four-foot line and seeing who can pitch his taw marble closest to the back line of the square. This is called lagging for first shot.

The object of the game is to get all the stone marbles by blasting them outside the square with the taw marbles. If a shooter blasts a stone marble (a man) from the square with his first shot during his turn, he may then continue to shoot until he misses. After each player's first shot of the game, which must be made from the four-foot line, all subsequent shots are made from where that player finds his taw marble when his turn comes up again.

The player shoots by holding his taw marble, which is usually an agate and somewhat smaller than the nine stone

118

marbles, in much the same manner as pennies are held for flipping. That is, the taw is held in the clenched fist between the thumb and the middle finger and then shot outward by the forward thrust of the player's thumb. Wrist or arm action is not permitted. Most shooting is done from a kneeling position.

When any player has knocked the last marble from the square, his opponent must put one of the original stone marbles, providing he has one, back in the field of play, thus providing a target for the player's next shot. A player can only put marbles back in the field of play that he has knocked out himself. When putting marbles back in field of play the player may place them anywhere on or within the square.

The game continues until one side has blasted all of the nine marbles from the square. Once one side has possession of all the stone men, that side is declared the winner.

If at any time, after each player's first shot, a player is able to blast his opponent's taw marble out of the field (square), said opponent must be able to put one of the original stone marbles back in field of play or the game is lost to him.

The ground rules may be altered with the players' prior consent. Sometimes the game is played so that it is possible to win by blasting the center man from the square with the first shot. At other times the game may be played allowing a player, whose taw has been blasted and who has none of the original stone marbles to put back in the game, one more shot, providing his opponent misses before clearing the field. If a player who has been given this allowance is able to knock one of the stone marbles from the field on his next shot, he must then put that marble back in play and proceed shooting until he misses. Then the game can continue as usual.

When the game is over the nine stone marbles are placed back in the tobacco sack, the string is pulled and the marbles are kept handy for the next game. The taws are carried by the individual players.

No Blade, No Trade

As I RECALL, nothing ever really stopped the whittling. Not heat—the men simply moved the kegs and crates to the shady side of the building. Not the cold—they moved the kegs and crates inside, around the pot-bellied stove. Not life itself!—a whole pack of male dogs fighting over Old Man Minick's blue tick bitch out in the dusty road might solicit only an occasional glance or a small side bet of a chaw of tobacco. Old Drum, Uncle Abe's prize coonhound, was the normal favorite.

Not even death stopped the whittling. Death might result in considerable silence with frequent glances at an empty keg, bench, or crate. And someone might say something such as, "Just seems like Abe is still settin' over there like he done sometimes—just whittlin' with that nickle-handled three-bladed stockman's knife that he traded off of Old Man Swafford that time."

The way I first heard the story of that great trade between Uncle Abe and Old Man Swafford (of course it changed as years went by), it was just before Christmas, on a rather cold Monday morning that Old Man Swafford first appeared around the (pot-bellied) stove at Humberd's General Store with his new knife. He sat down on a nail keg (many later said it was a tomato crate) amidst sacks and barrels of pinto beans, navy beans, brown sugar, white sugar, salt pork, flour, meal, and horehound candy and he took out that nickle-handled three-bladed stockman's knife, which, he said, he bought while peddling apples in Fort Smith that fall.

It was later that same day (everybody agrees on that) that Uncle Abe came down to the store. (Uncle Abe always gave as evidence that he must have come in last for he had worked his traps before he had come down. The reason he hadn't sat down right away was because he was cold so he had stood there with his backside to the stove for a while.)

According to Uncle Abe it was the same year when the itch was so bad. But most everyone else disagreed with that. Others said that there wasn't hardly any itch at all around that year. But Uncle Abe argued that there was a good deal of itch around, for he could always remember how good his itch had felt while he was standing there next to that hot stove looking down at Old Man Swafford's new knife.

Uncle Abe always recalled that his hands were very cold, so he hadn't started to whittle right away even when he sat down. And besides, he wanted to build up as much suspense as possible before he brought out his own five-bladed bone-handled barlow knife which he had bought that fall in Denver while working in the broomcorn harvest. (Some contend, even today, that Uncle Abe actually purchased that knife in Dodge City while working in the wheat harvest during the summer. Joe Adcock even goes so far as to insist that he was there, with Uncle Abe, when he bought it, and Joe always cinches the argument by saying, "You can buy a darn good knife in Dodge City.")

Uncle Abe always said that *he* sat down on a hogshead of blackstrap molasses about a quarter of the way around the stove from Old Man Swafford. (Tom Humberd always remembered that Uncle Abe sat on a barrel, nothing so big as a hogshead, but he did remember thinking then that Abe had the better seat for trading. Uncle Abe allowed that such a decided advantage might be unfair in any other sport, but he figured that knife-swapping was about a fifth sleight of hand, one-fifth luck, one-fifth deceit and two-fifths patience.)

It was obvious from the beginning who had the biggest knife. That didn't mean very much, but still it was something. Uncle Abe's bigger and *better* knife made Old Man Swafford whittle a little faster and the shavings were much thicker than normal. Uncle Abe recollected being very pleased to see this change. It had been more than he had hoped for. (Uncle Abe later said that Swafford acted like a nanny goat that had backed into a blackberry bush.)

Old Man Swafford always maintained publicly that he had left the store right away because Uncle Abe had smelled the place all up with polecat scent. But Uncle Abe insisted that this could not have been the case for it had been the next day that he had come in smelling that way and, "it weren't a polecat nohow—it were a skunk." He remembered this because polecats were worth only about thirty-five cents and he had gotten a dollar-fifty for that hide. Old Tom Humberd says that Uncle Abe was right about the day he had come in smelling that way, but that he was wrong about it being a skunk. Tom remembered buying the hide for twenty-five cents and selling it to the hide-buyer for thirty-five cents.

Anyway, everyone agrees that Old Man Swafford rushed home. Tom Humberd followed him and says to this day that the old man didn't even stop at the house but went directly to the outhouse. Now, going to the outhouse had been a dead giveaway, since he never used it for the usual purpose. New-fangled outhouses was for the women folks. But it was the place where he could find the Sears and Roebuck catalog and find out how much Uncle Abe's knife was worth.

In the days that followed both men sat whittling quietly, occasionally shaving some hair off their respective arms or holding a horsehair up in the long winter rays of the sun and splitting it deftly. There were sudden games of solitary mumble peg where the knife was retrieved almost before it hit the floor. I am told, on good authority, that Uncle Abe made shavings so thin they floated in mid-air. And not to be outdone, Old Man Swafford, by carving around and around a fine piece of white pine, made a one-half inch shaving that was ninety-five feet long, give or take some. (This had actually been measured one evening after the old man had gone home to see what the old woman had cooked up.)

But Uncle Abe didn't spend all his time whittling. Uncle Abe—and this is to his credit—hadn't lied about where he had been spending some of his time. He said that he had been working in his blacksmith shop. He said something about it going to be time for spring planting afore anyone knew it, and now was a good time to get your tools in shape—be greening up one of these days. This sort of conversation seemed to make everyone uneasy so they had not pursued it. But they wondered what was getting into Uncle Abe. Even so, a good

"Man ought to have something to trade, seems like," Old Man Swafford observed.

"Does seem thataway, don't it? I been thinking a little about maybe trading for a hound pup—seeing as how Old Drum ain't gettin' any younger. I want to use Old Drum to train him. But I think I will wait a year or two." Uncle Abe had seemed, to those who heard him, to almost fáll asleep while talking.

Even so, such an admission had seemed to the experienced traders as a blunder on the part of Uncle Abe. Old Man Swafford appeared to others as if he'd treed a coon. The very next day Old Man Swafford came back to whittle, bringing with him one of the best looking he-pups he owned. But even though that pup was the spitting image of Old Drum (probably was his son, in fact), Uncle Abe hardly gave it the second look. He seemed to have forgotten entirely his interest in a hound pup from the day before.

They say it was unbelievable the antics that Old Man Swafford put that pup through. He tied tin cans to its tail. He blew in the pup's big ears. He made shoes out of paper candy sacks and fastened them to the pup's huge feet. He had it chasing a kitten all over the store. Every time the awkward pup came by he would stick his foot out and trip it, making it fall all over itself. All day long that pup was the center of attention. But Uncle Abe hardly noticed it at all.

It was late that afternoon before serious bartering got underway.

"What you got to trade on?" Old Man Swafford asked the question again as if he were saying, "How's the family?"

"Nothing you'd want, I'd 'spect."

Both men had stopped whittling and had put their knives in their pockets. The others continued to whittle and pretended not to notice what was going on. Old Man Swafford had the pup up in his lap now. He would stretch out one and then the other long ear of the pup. Uncle Abe got up and scratched himself against a brace pole as if he were about to leave. Swafford took one of the pup's huge feet and spread it out upon his knee.

part of each day was spent in whittling, neat piles of shavings accumulating on the floor, as the tension over the two new knives mounted.

It was Old Man Swafford who finally got impatient. Everyone agreed that that had been his undoing. "He ought to of just held on and let Abe take the lead," they said.

"Got anything to trade on?" Old Man Swafford asked just as calm as you please.

"Naw, nothing worth mentioning, ain't done much swapping lately, been too busy—working in the shop, my traps and all." Uncle Abe changed ends with the stick he was whittling on and started cutting notches.

"Shore getting late," Uncle Abe said, looking out at the sun.

Now, the way Old Man Swafford had it figured, he would be getting a little bit the better of the trade if he could swap his knife and the pup for Uncle Abe's knife. But instead of offering the pup right away, Old Man Swafford says, "Trade you knives sight unseen if you'll throw in a boar pig from that new litter you got." This gesture by Swafford had been expected by everyone.

Uncle Abe took his time, seemed to be giving the matter some serious thought. "Naw, I wouldn't be interested in that," he said.

"I'm going to need a brute by next year. This is a mighty fine knife. You can't buy a better one in the whole state." Old Man Swafford took the knife out of his pocket and held it sort of loose-like in his fist.

"Maybe not—not in Arkansas anyway. But I think I'll just keep the knife I got in Denver." Uncle Abe took his knife out too, and held it in such a way as to be barely visible to Swafford.

"Tell you what I'll do. I'll trade you knives sight unseen and if'n you'll throw in the pig I'll throw in this here pup." Everyone agreed that Swafford seemed far too eager.

Uncle Abe took a surprisingly long time to consider this. "Naw, I think I'll wait about the pup. And I'm satisfied with my knife anyway. Maybe you can trade that knife off to somebody else."

Both men were still holding their knives so they could be partly seen through their fingers. Uncle Abe had actually started to walk off when Old Man Swafford made the final offer. "All right, I'll trade you knives sight unseen and I'll give you this pup to boot. And that is it. That's the trade."

Uncle Abe concentrated for only a moment this time. He held out his hand with the knife in it. "You want to trade this knife for that knife you're a-holdin' and you'll give the pup to boot?"

"That's the trade." It was obvious that this was Old Man Swafford's final offer.

"No blade, no trade," Abe said, holding out his left hand with the knife partially concealed in it.

"No blade, no trade," Old Man Swafford agreed.

The two men shook hands as they exchanged knives and Swafford handed over the pup.

No two people agree on what happened after that. Some said that Old Man Swafford simply took Abe's knife, looked at it, and went home. Others said that he sat right down and started in whittling as if nothing had happened. Some said that he looked sick, while others said he had a fixed smile on his face. One person said later that they had heard him say, "Well, I'll be dogged." Some thought that he had actually cussed, but few people believed that.

For some time after that Uncle Abe took turns with the knives. One day he would whittle with the barlow knife which he said he had bought in Denver, the next day he would whittle with the stockman's knife which he had gotten off Old Man Swafford by trading him that home-made replica with the old straight razor blade in it.

128

133

Afterword

List of Etchings and Drawings

(with original size in centimeters)

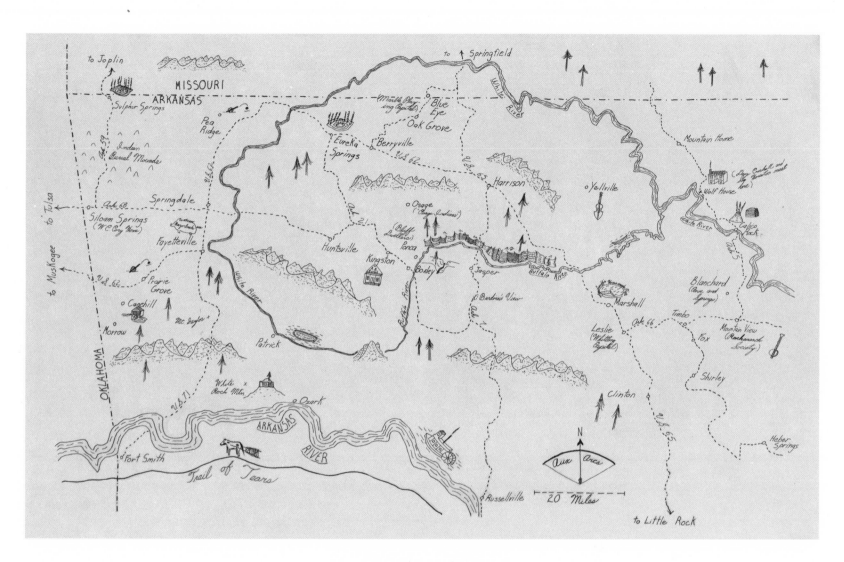

The Ozarks of Arkansas

Acknowledgments

HERE ARE ONLY A FEW of the many folk in the Ozarks I wish to acknowledge
for helping this project become a reality:

> Tom and Edna Lowe, for that wonderful year
>   Joyce and I spent in their rent cottage
> Uncle Glen and Aunt Elizabeth Loftin, for
>   shelter and good downhome cooking
> Jean and Tommy Simmons, for introducing us
>   to the music of the Ozarks
> Jack Moncrief, for making his darkroom
>   available during the Guggenheim year
> Harrison and Agnes Pierce, for allowing us
>   to camp out on their land and for their
>   spirit of trust and cooperation
> Uncle Dow Abshier, for introducing me to some of
>   the nooks and crannies of the Ozarks
> Aunt Geneva Waterman, for helping us come up
>   with the title *Hills of Home*
> Vance Randolph, for teaching us all so much
>   about the Ozarks through his writings
> Grandma (Mary) Abshier, for giving me some of
>   my most vivid memories of the old home place
>   during my childhood
> Grandma (Nora) Minick, for that snowed-in week
>   in 1970 filled with stories and hot sassafras tea

Others who contributed in various ways to further the Ozark project
are: Matt and Gesa Kearney, for loan of a car to make a trip to the Ozarks
in 1968; Margaretta and Frederick Mitchell for their continued encouragement; Dorothy Abshier Minick, who, with my father, introduced me
to the Ozarks in the first place.

I would like to extend my special appreciation to my father and Leonard
Sussman for agreeing to participate in this project when there was no cer-
tainty of a book.

Last, I wish to thank Joyce for her love and sustained enthusiasm
for the project and for her fresh eye when it came to choosing the right
photographs.

Roger Minick
Berkeley, 1975

Body type is Monotype Baskerville by Peters Typesetting
Display type is Baskerville and Baskerville Light by Spartan Typographers
Presswork for *Hills of Home* was completed in June, 1975
at Phelps/Schaefer in San Francisco
Binding by Cardoza-James
Design by Roger Minick with Leonard Sussman and Frederick Mitchell
Production: Dick Schuettge and Georgia George